Anonymous

The student's manual of Maráthí grammar : designed for high schools

Anonymous

The student's manual of Maráthí grammar : designed for high schools

ISBN/EAN: 9783337156886

Printed in Europe, USA, Canada, Australia, Japan

Cover: Foto ©Paul-Georg Meister /pixelio.de

More available books at **www.hansebooks.com**

THE
STUDENT'S MANUAL

OF

MARÁṬHÍ GRAMMAR.

(DESIGNED FOR HIGH SCHOOLS.)

𝔅𝔬𝔪𝔟𝔞𝔶:

PRINTED AT THE
EDUCATION SOCIETY'S PRESS, BYCULLA.

1868.

[*The Copyright and Right of Translation are reserved.*]

PREFACE.

The following pages were first written by me for the benefit of my own pupils, who were preparing for Matriculation, as they could not find all the needful information in the existing treatises on Maráthí Grammar. Believing that they might prove useful to other students, I have ventured to publish them; and should scholars, who may chance to see them, suggest any improvements, I shall feel grateful.

I have paid special attention to simplicity and perspicuity in the composition of this book, and have on this account abstained from all allusion to Sanskrit and other languages, except in the chapters on derivation. I have treated of the several departments of Grammar separately, which may have the effect of setting this intricate subject in a clear and interesting form before the student. I have earnestly sought to unfold and evolve the laws and principles of the Maráthí language, rather than engraft those of other languages on it, but how far I have succeeded in my attempts I leave it to the public to judge.

The classification of the laws of the changes of vowels and consonants, which take place in inflection and composition; the division of the verbs into conjugations; the systematic arrangement of the compounds under three classes, and the observations on the obscure and apparent compounds, the formation of the vocables, &c. &c., are quite new and original. The chapter on the origin of the inflections cannot fail to interest the student. It is, indeed, a most important discovery which philologists have made, that the inflections, which were looked upon but a few years back as meaningless particles, are words or fragments of words; it has thrown a flood of interesting light upon the whole subject of Grammar. The Maráthí language fully confirms this discovery: the personal-ending तो in करितो He does, is the veritable demonstrative pronoun तो that; the dative termination ला is identical with लागीं.

I am deeply indebted in the composition of this book to Dr. STEVENSON's *Maráṭhí Grammar*. The grammatical forms which he gives have the sanction of the learned Shástrís who assisted our two great lexicographers in the compilation of their Dictionaries, and have been, moreover, adopted by the Government Educational Department. My observations on the declensions, tenses, &c. are entirely based upon his, and I believe I should, perhaps, have never been able to write a single line without the aid of his book. Mr. MOLESWORTH's *Maráṭhí and English Dictionary* has furnished me with valuable information on various points, particularly on the spelling and the duplicatives. The Grammars of Mr. DA'DOBA' PA'NDURANG and Mr. KRISHNA SHA'STRI' GODBOLE have rendered me great assistance, while a number of smaller works in the Maráṭhí and Gujarátí languages have been profitably consulted.

Very valuable has been the help which I have received from several Sanskrit, Greek, and English grammars in the arrangement of my subject-matter, and if my book is indeed clear and systematic, the credit is due to those books rather than to me. I would, however, make particular mention of two European authors, whose books have done me great service in the department of derivation : I mean MAX MÜLLER and Dr. ANGUS.

The importance of a critical knowledge of a language cannot be overrated ; for words exercise a powerful influence upon thought and science in general. "Men believe," says Lord Bacon, "that their reason is lord over their words ; but it happens, too, that words exercise a reciprocal and reactionary power over our intellect."

The moral influence of the study of languages is highly beneficial. In establishing a relationship between distant and dissimilar languages, philology teaches us to recognize in every fellow-man a brother. This noble truth of the brotherhood of humanity was, no doubt, first propounded by the Hebrew sages of old, but comparative philology has the honour of confirming it, and giving it an authority and currency in the learned world.

TABLE OF CONTENTS.

ORTHOGRAPHY.

	PAGE
CHAPTER I.—Letters and Sounds	1
CHAPTER II.—Combination of Letters...............	5
I. Syllabification of Letters	5
II. Sandhi or Rules for the Union of Letters in Sanskṛit words....................	7
III. Vowel changes in Maráṭhí words	10
Note.—Rules for Spelling	12

ETYMOLOGY.

CHAPTER III.—General Observations on the Classification and Inflection of Words....	14
CHAPTER IV.—Substantives	15
I. Cases of Substantives..................	16
II. Numbers of Substantives	19
III. Gender of Substantives	21
CHAPTER V.—Declension of Substantives	25
First Declension............................	28
Second Declension.........................	30
Third Declension	31
Fourth Declension.........................	33
Fifth Declension...........................	34
Sixth Declension...........................	35
CHAPTER VI.—Adjectives.	
Adjectives of Quality	39
Numerals	41
CHAPTER VII.—Pronouns.	
Personal Pronouns........................	47
Reflexive Pronouns.......................	49
Relative Pronouns	50
Demonstrative Pronouns	51
Interrogative Pronouns	53
Indefinite Pronouns	55

CHAPTER VIII.—Adverbs (Declinable)............	55
CHAPTER IX.—The Verb	56
I.—The Classification of Verbs	56
II.—The Inflection of Verbs............	57
Tenses........................	58
Moods........................	60
Verbal Nouns and Participles	61
Constructions	64
Voices........................	66
CHAPTER X.—Conjugation.................	67
First Conjugation	68
Second Conjugation	68
The Personal-Endings	69
Paradigms (1st and 2nd Conj.)	72
CHAPTER XI.—Conjugation *continued*.	
The Potential Verb	75
The Causal Verb...................	77
The Irregular Verb	78
The Anomalous Verb	81
The Substantive Verb	82
The Negative Substantive Verb	88
The Defective Verb.................	90
The Compound Verb	91
CHAPTER XII.—Compound Tenses	92
The Indicative Mood	93
The Conditional Mood	95
The Subjunctive Mood	97
The Participles	97
Compound Negative Tenses	98
The Passive Voice	99
CHAPTER XIII.—Particles, or Indeclinable Words.	100
I. The Adverb	100
II. The Preposition	102
III. The Conjunction	103
IV. The Interjection	103

CHAPTER XIV.—DERIVATION 104
    I. Primary Derivatives 108
    II. Secondary Derivatives:—
        Prefixes 110
        Suffixes....................... 112
    III. Reduplicatives................. 115
    IV. Compounds 117
        I. True Compounds............ 117
            Substantive Compounds....... 118
            Adjective Compounds 121
            Adverbial Compounds......... 122
        II. Obscure Compounds 122
        III. Apparent Compounds........... 124

CHAPTER XV.—THE STRUCTURE OF GRAMMATICAL
        FORMS 124
        Pronouns......................... 124
        Verbs........................... 125
        Adverbs......................... 125
        Postpositions 127
        Conjunctions 128
        Interjections 129

CHAPTER XVI.—INFLECTIONS..................... 129
    I. Noun Inflections................. 129
    II. Verbal Inflections 133

APPENDIX.

    I. Note on Old Maráṭhí Grammatical Forms. 138
    II. Note on Parsing 139

THE STUDENT'S MANUAL
OF
MARÁTHÍ GRAMMAR.

1.—Grammar treats of the principles of language, and Maráthí Grammar of the principles of the Maráthí language.

2. The principles of every language are based either on the laws of thought, or general usage.

3. Written language consists of letters, words, and sentences, and Grammar is, accordingly, divided into Orthography, Etymology, and Syntax.

CHAPTER I.
ORTHOGRAPHY.
LETTERS AND SOUNDS.

ORTHOGRAPHY treats of the sounds and powers of letters.

4. The Maráthí letters (वर्ण) are thus written and pronounced :—

Vowels

अ	a (as in Roman)
आ	á (as in father.)
इ	i (as in sit.)
ई	í (as in Police.)
उ	u (as in put.)
ऊ	ú (as in rude.)
ऋ	ri (as in rid.)
ॠ	rí (as in read.)
ऌ	li (as in lid.)

ऌ	li (as in lead.)
ए	e (as in there.)
ऐ	ai (as in aisle or the Italian mai.)
ओ	o (as in so.)
औ	au (as ow in now.)
क	ka (like k in king.)
ख	kha (like kh in khan.)
ग	ga (like g in give.)
घ	gha (like gh in Afghan.)
ङ	ṅa (like ng in sing.)
च	cha (like ch in church; also ts.)
छ	chha (like ch+h; also ts+h.)
ज	ja (like j in jet; also dz.)
झ	jha (like j+h; also dz+h.)
ञ	ña (like n in singe.)
ट	ṭa (like t in trumpet.)
ठ	ṭha (like t+h.)
ड	ḍa (like d in drain.)
ढ	ḍha (like d+h.)
ण	ṇa (like n in country.)
त	ta (like t in tube.)
थ	tha (like th in thin.)
द	da (like d in due.)
ध	dha (like d+h.)
न	na (like n in then.)
प	pa (like p in push.)
फ	pha (like ph in up-hill.)
ब	ba (like b in bag.)
भ	bha (b+h.)
म	ma (like m in man.)
य	ya (like y in you.)
र	ra (like r in Rome.)

ल	*la*	(like *l* in live.)
व	*va*	(like *v* and *w* in vein and were.)
श	*s'a*	(like *ss* in session.)
ष	*sha*	(like *sh* in shun.)
स	*sa*	(like *s* in son.)
ह	*ha*	(like *h* in hand.)
ळ	*la*	
क्ष	*ksha*	(like *ctio* in diction.)
ज्ञ	*dnya*	

Note.—The letters down to म are *systematically* arranged in several classes, and those from य to ज्ञ are *miscellaneous* letters.

5. Of these letters fourteen are *Vowels* (स्वर) अ, आ, इ, ई, उ, ऊ, ऋ, ॠ, लृ, लॄ, ए, ऐ, ओ, औ, and the rest are *Consonants* (व्यंजनें).

6. Vowels are divided into *short* (ऱ्हस्व) and *long* vowels (दीर्घ), and *diphthongs* (संयुक्त स्वर).

The short vowels are अ, इ, उ, ऋ, लृ; the long are आ, ई, ऊ, ॠ, लॄ, and the remaining letters are diphthongs, ए, ऐ, ओ, औ.

The long vowels are each composed of two similar, and the diphthongs of two dissimilar vowels.

Thus, आ = अ + अ; ई = इ + इ; ऊ = उ + उ; ॠ = ऋ + ऋ; लॄ = लृ + लृ.

ए = अ or आ + इ or ई;   ओ = अ or आ + उ or ऊ;
ऐ = अ or आ + ए;   औ = अ or आ + ओ.

Of the diphthongs ऐ and औ are *proper diphthongs* (वृद्धि), and ए and ओ are *improper diphthongs* (गुण).

7. Besides these vowels, there are *semi-vowels* (अंतःस्थ), which are included among the consonants, य, र, ल, व. They are thus formed:—

य = इ or ई + अ;   र = ऋ or ऋ + अ;
ल = लृ or लॄ + अ;   व = उ or ऊ + अ.

8. A consonant cannot be sounded without a vowel, as ब् *b*, pronounced as ब *ba*.

9. Consonants are divided according to the *position* (स्थान) of the mouth where they are produced, into *five* classes:—

    1. *Gutturals* or throat sounds (कंठ्य):—
       क्, ख्, ग्, घ्, ङ्, ह्.

    2. *Palatals*, or palate sounds (तालव्य):—
       च्, छ्, ज्, झ्, ञ्, य्, श्.

    3. *Cerebrals*, or brain sounds (मूर्धन्य):—
       ट्, ठ्, ड्, ढ्, ण्, र्, ष्, ळ्.

    4. *Dentals*, or teeth sounds (दंत्य):—
       त्, थ्, द्, ध्, न्, ल्, स्.

    5. *Labials*, or lip sounds, (ओष्ठ्य):—
       प्, फ्, ब्, भ्, म्, व्.

Consonants are also divided according to their *power* (प्रयत्न), that is, whether they can be pronounced with or without a vowel, into *mutes* (स्पर्श), and *semivocals* (ईषद्विवृत). The vowels are *vocals* (विवृत).

10. The *mutes* are subdivided into—

    Hard or *surd* (अघोष) क्, च्, ट्, त्, प् ⎫
    Soft or *sonant* (घोषवत्) ग्, ज्, ड्, द्, ब् ⎬ Unaspirated (अल्पप्राण).
    Aspirate (महाप्राण) ख्, घ्, छ्, झ्, ठ्, ढ्, थ्, ध्, फ्, भ्.

Note.—The aspirated consonants contain each an unaspirated consonant and ह्: ख्=क्+ह्.

11. The *semivocals* are subdivided into—

    Liquids (अंतःस्थ) य्, र्, ल्, व्.
    Nasals (अनुनासिक) ङ्, ञ्, ण्, न्, म्.
    Sibilants (ऊष्म) श्, ष्, स्, ह्.

The consonants क्ष and ज्ञ are double letters, besides which there are several others in the language.

12. अं or ‒ is called *Anusvára*, and अः or: is *Visarga*.

The *Anusvára* represents a nasal sound, and the *Visarga* is an aspirate.

13. The *Anusvára* is pronounced before the consonants like the nasals of the class to which they belong, *e. g.*, before a guttural like the nasal of the guttural class, &c. Thus—

भंग = अङ्ग	corresponding to the nasal			ङ्.
भंजन = भञ्जन	,,	,,	,,	ञ्.
दंडन = दण्डन	,,	,,	,,	ण्.
अंत = अन्त	,,	,,	,,	न्.
सांव = साम्ब	,,	,,	,,	म्.

Before र्, श्, ष, स्, ह्, and ज्ञ, the *Anusvára* assumes merely the sound of *nv*, without taking the letters; as संरक्षण = सं(व्)रक्षण = *Sanvrakshaṇa*.

Before य्, ल्, and व् the *Anusvára* doubles the semivowels, retaining at the same time a slight nasalization: thus—

संयोग = सय्यँोग Sayyoga
संलग्न = सल्लँग्न Sallagna
संवाद = सव्वँाद Savváda.

When the *Anusvára* is put, in pure Maráṭhí words, upon a long vowel followed by a hard letter, as काँटा a thorn, or on a long vowel at the end of a word, as उठणें to rise, it has only a slight nasal sound. This slight nasal sound of the *Anusvára* is called अनुनासिक or *Anunásika*.

CHAPTER II.

ON THE COMBINATION OF LETTERS.

I. The Syllabification of Letters (अक्षरें).

14. When a vowel combines with a consonant, it is marked by a different sign, placed before or after, above or below, the consonant after which it is pronounced. This combination of the vowels with the consonants is called बारासकडीं, or बाराखडीं, twelve links.

The forms which the vowels assume are the following:—

ा (आ) ि (इ) ी (ई) ु (उ) ू (ऊ) े (ए) ै (ऐ) ो (ओ) ौ (औ)
का कि की कु कू के कै को कौ

When अ combines with a consonant, the consonant drops the *virāma* (्) at the foot of it, as क् k becomes क ka: the अ is said to be *inherent* in क ka.

Some consonants alter their forms when combined with the vowels:—

र + उ = रु; र + ऊ = रू.
श + उ = शु; श + ऊ = शू.
श + ऋ = शृ; श + ॠ = शॄ.

15. When the consonants are combined, they are written with one consonant placed under the other, omitting the transverse line of the lower, as in ह्ह (ह्ह), or by placing the one after the other and dropping the perpendicular line of the first, as in ज्य (जय). The double consonants are called जोड़ाक्षरें, double letters.

The following are a few of the principal double letters:—

क्क	k-ka	ग्न	g-na	च्म	ch-ma	ण्ण	ṇ-ṇa
क्त	k-ta	ग्र	g-ra	च्छ्र	ch-chhra	ण्म	ṇ-ma
क्त्व	k-tva	ग्र्य	g-r-ya	ज्ज	j-ja	र्ण्य	r-ṇ-ya
क्न	k-na	ग्ल	g-la	ज्र	j-ra	त्त	t-ta
क्म	k-ma	घ्य	gh-ya	ज्व	j-va	त्य	t-ya
क्र	k-ra	घ्र	gh-ra	ट्ट	ṭ-ṭa	त्र	t-ra
क्य	k-ya	घ्व	gh-va	ट्य	ṭ-ya	त्प्र	t-p-ra
क्ल	k-la	घ्न	gh-na	ठ्र	ṭh-ra	त्स	t-sa
क्व	k-va	ङ्क	ṅ-ka	ठ्य	ṭh-ya	त्र्य	t-r-ya
क्ष	k-sha	ङ्क्त	ṅ-k-ta	ड्ग	ḍ-ga	त्स्य	t-s-ya
क्ष्य	k-shya	च्य	ch-ya	ड्य	ḍ-ya	त्थ	t-tha
क्ष्व	k-shva	च्च	ch-cha	ड्व	ḍ-va	त्स्न	t-s-na
ख्य	kh-ya	च्छ	ch-chha	ड्म	ḍ-ma	त्त्र	t-t-ra
ग्ध	g-dha	च्छ्व	ch-chhva	ढ्य	ḍh-ya	थ्य	th-ya

(7)

ग्र	d-ga	स्प	p-sa	ल्य	l-ya	ष्ठ	sh-ṭha
द्व	d-va	प्न	p-na	ल्प	l-pa	ष्ठ्य	sh-ṭh-ya
द्य	d-ya	प्य	p-ya	ल्म	l-ma	ष्प	sh-pa
द्द	d-da	प्म	p-ma	ल्ल	l-la	ष्ण	sh-ṇa
द्र्य	d-r-ya	प्ल	p-la	व्य	v-ya	ष्य	sh-ya
द्ब	d-ba	प्र	p-ra	व्र	v-ra	स्क	s-ka
द्ब्र	d-b-ra	ब्ध	b-dha	श्र	s'-ra	स्ख	s-kha
द्व्य	d-v-ya	ब्र	b-ra	श्न	s'-na	स्त	s-ta
द्र	d-ra	भ्य	bh-ya	श्य	s'-ya	स्र	s-ra
द्म	d-ma	भ्र	bh-ra	श्ल	s'-la	स्फ	s-pha
द्भ	d-bha	भ्ण	bh-ṇa	श्व	s'-va	स्य	s-ya
ध्ध	dh-dha	भ्व	bh-va	श्च	s'-cha	ण्ह	ṇ-ha
ध्न	dh-na	भ्न	bh-na	ष्क	sh-ka	ह्म	h-ma
ध्र	dh-ra	म्र	m-ra	ष्क्र	sh k-ra	न्ह	n-ha
ध्य	dh-ya	म्व	m-va	ष्ट	sh-ṭa	ह्य	h-ya
र्ध्व	r-dh-va	म्म	m-ma	ष्ट्र	sh-ṭ-ra	ह्र	h-ra
न्न	n-na	य्व	y-va	ष्ट्व	sh-ṭ-va	ह्व	h-va
प्त	p-ta	ल्क	l-ka	ष्ट्य	sh-ṭ-ya	ह्ल	h-la

16. The mark, called *virāma*, pause, which denotes the absence of a vowel, is placed at the foot of a consonant, as अकस्मात् *akasmát*.

Note.—In Maráṭhi the final consonant of a word has no अ inherent in it,—*e. g.*, हात्—though the *viráma* is not subscribed, and hence हात् is a monosyllable.

II. Sandhi, or Rules for the Union of Letters in Sanskrit Words.

17. The rules of *Sandhi* are applicable chiefly to the combination of letters in Sanskrit words, and may be thus briefly stated :—

18. I. The combination of vowels is called अच्संधि (*Ach Sandhi*).

(1) Two similar vowels, short or long, coalesce into their corresponding *long vowel*: वस्त्र + अन्न = वस्त्रान्न food and clothes; धर्म + आश्रय = धर्माश्रय; हरि + इच्छा = हरीच्छा; करी + इंद्र = करींद्र; भानु + उदय = भानूदय.

(2) If अ or आ be followed by a dissimilar vowel, the two

vowels coalesce into their corresponding *improper diphthong*: परम + ईश्वर = परमेश्वर the Supreme Lord.

(3) If अ or आ be followed by a diphthong, either proper or improper, the vowels coalesce into their corresponding *proper diphthongs*: रक्त + ओघ = रक्तौघ flow of blood.

(4) If a simple vowel (*i. e.* not diphthongal), with the exception of अ or आ, be followed by a dissimilar vowel, whether simple or diphthongal, the former is changed to its coresponding *semivowel*: जाति + आधार = जात्याधार, the support of caste.

(5) If the improper diphthongs ए and ओ are followed by any vowel, simple or diphthongal (except अ), they are changed into अय् and अव् respectively (combined with the other vowel): चे + अन = चयन selection गो + इंद्र = गवेंद्र lord of kine (Krishṇa), &c. *Exc.* गो + अक्ष = गवाक्ष, a window (literally a bull's eye).

(6) If the proper diphthongs ऐ and औ be followed by any vowel, simple or diphthongal, आय् and आव् are respectively substituted (combined with the other vowels): नै + अक = नायक a chief; नौ + इक = नाविक naval.

19. II. The combination of consonants is called हल्संधि.

(1) For the purpose of combination, the letters of the alphabet are divided into *two great* classes, viz. *Surds* (hard) and *Sonants* (soft): thus—

Surds.	Sonants.
क्, ख्,	ग्, घ्, ङ्, अ, आ, ए, ऐ
च्, छ्, श्,	ज्, झ्, ञ्, य्, इ, ई
ट् ठ् ष्	ड्, ढ्, ण्, र्, ऋ, ॠ,
त् थ् स	द्, ध्, न्, ल्, व् ल् ल्,
प्, फ् The *Visarga*.	ब्, भ्, म्, उ, ऊ, ओ, औ The *Anusvara*.

20. When two consonants combine, they undergo either a change of *quality*, or a change of *quality, and place*.

When a surd is changed to a sonant, or a sonant to a surd, the consonant is said to undergo *a change of quality*; जगत् + ईश = जगद् + ईश = जगदीश lord of the world.

When a consonant of one organ or place is substituted by a consonant of another organ, it is said to undergo *a change of place*: सत् + शास्त्र = सच् + शास्त्र = सच्छास्त्र the true scripture.

21. The following two rules relate to consonantal *changes of quality*:—

1. The first consonant of two uniting consonants, if a surd, is changed to its corresponding sonant, when the second is a sonant: षट् + रिपु = षड्रिपु.

2. The first consonant of two uniting consonants, if a sonant, is changed to a surd, if the second is a surd: क्षुध् + विपासा = क्षुत् + विपासा or क्षुत्पिपासा hunger and thirst.

Note. It is the *second* letter that has the assimilating power.

Note. The nasals do not undergo a change in quality.

Note. When the first consonant undergoes a change, it, though an aspirate, is changed only to its corresponding unaspirate; क्षुध् + विपासा = क्षुत् + विपासा, not क्षुथ् + विपासा.

22. The consonants that undergo a change of place are chiefly *the dentals, the nasals,* and *the sibilants*.

The dentals, न, थ, द, ध, become palatals before the palatals, च, छ, ज, झ, ञ, श, and cerebrals, before the cerebrals, ट, ठ, ड, ढ, ण (not ष): as सत् + जन = सच् + जन = सज्जन; भवत् + उमह् = भवट् + उमह् = भवडुमह्.

The dentals before ल are changed to ल्, बृहत् + ललाट = बृहल् + ललाट = बृहल्ललाट a large forehead.

The dentals, as well as all other consonants, are changed to their corresponding nasals, before the nasals; जगत् + नाथ = जगद् + नाथ or

जगन् + नाथ = जगन्नाथ lord of the world; दिक् + नाग = दिङ्नाग a world elephant.

The *visarga* before a sibilant may or may not be changed into the sibilant that is before it; दुः + शासन = दुःशासन or दुश्शासन.

The *visarga* before a sonant is generally changed to र्; कविः + अयं = कविरयं this poet.

The dental न् before च and छ requires the intervention of श्; before त and श the intervention of स्; and before ट and ष the intervention of ष्; पतन् + तरु = पतन् + स्तरु = पतंस्तरु a falling tree.

न् before ज, झ, ञ, and श is changed to ञ्; तान् + जयति = ताञ्जयति, he conquers them; before ट, ठ, ड, ढ, ण, to ण्; and before ल to ल्; महान् + लाभ = महाल्लाभ large gain.

Note. न after ऋ, ॠ, र्, ष, is changed into ण; भाप + अन = भापण.

III. Vowel Changes in Maráthí Words.

23. Vowels undergo a change in Maráthí, either when words are inflected, or when two or more words are combined to form one word.

24. 1. *Vowel changes required by Inflection.*

(1) When two vowels unite, the latter is substituted for the former. Thus,

भट + ईण = भटीण, a Bráhman woman. ⎫ Gender termina-
देशपांड्या + ईण = देशपांडीण. ⎭ tions.

घर = ईं = घरीं ⎫ Case terminations.
in a house ⎭

कर + ऊन = करून, having done. ⎫ Vowel terminations.
कर + आवें = करावें, should do, &c. ⎭

(2) If the word which is inflected be a monosyllable, like ने carry, घे take, पी drink, &c., both the uniting vowels retain a place in the word. Thus,

ने + ऊन = नेऊन having taken.

पी + ऊं = पीऊं to drink.

पी + आवें = प्यांवें may drink.

जा + ओ = जाओ or जावो may he go, &c.

(3) When a word ending in a short इ or उ is inflected the final इ or उ is lengthened. Thus,

मति + स = मतीस to reason.

भानु + नें = भानूनें by the sun, &c.

(4) When a word is inflected, the penultimate, or the vowel preceding the final vowel, is shortened. This is the case when the penultimate is ई or ऊ. Thus,

पीठ + स = पिठास to flour.

ऊठ + तों = उठतों I arise.

बारीक + आई = बारिकाई thinness.

Note. Sometimes, the penultimate is changed to अ or its corresponding semi-vowel य or व्. Thus,

उंदीर + स = उंदि or -दरास to a rat.

गाइर + ईण = गाइ or -यरीण to a female singer.

दऊत + नें = दउ or -वतोनें to an inkstand.

Note. The penultimate of Sanskrit and other foreign words may or may not be shortened; thus नीति, नीतीनें or नितोनें by morality.

25. II. *Vowel Changes required by Composition :—*

(1) When two vowels unite in composition, if the first be any other vowel than अ, it generally displaces the second vowel. Thus,

खिडकी + आंतून = खिडकींतून from a window.

करिनो + आहे = करिनोहे he is doing.

(2) But when the first vowel is अ, and the second is some other vowel, the first is displaced, but then the displacing vowel drops its own consonant, and assumes that of the other vowel. Thus,

एरंड + तेल = एरंडेल castor oil.

आंबट + घाण = आंबटाण sour smell.

Note. These vowel changes chiefly take place in the *Obscure Compounds* (Sec. 152).

NOTE. *Rules for Spelling.*

The Anusvára is never replaced by another letter before र, व, श, ष, स, ह, ञ ; as संरक्षण, and never संवरक्षण, protection.

The Anusvára may or may not be put in Maráṭhí words on long vowels followed by the letters य, र, ल, व, श, ष, स, ह, ळ ; as भोंसकणें or भोसकणें to pierce ; वासरुं or वासरु, a calf.

The Anusvára is always used in the following words :—

Upon the last letter of every neuter noun, whether singular or plural; as मोतीं a pearl, मोत्यें pearls.

Upon the penultimate of a plural noun when it is inflected ; माणसांचा of a man, माणसांचा of men.

Upon the third case-endings and the seventh case-endings; as नें by, ईं in, &c.

Upon the sixth case-endings when governed by a neuter noun; as याचें घर his house.

Upon the final letters of numerals above one hundred, denoting hundreds, thousands, &c., as सातशें seven hundred, हजारों thousands.

Upon the second personal pronoun तूं, and its instrumental singular and plural forms; त्वां by thee.

Upon the instrumental forms of the first personal pronoun; as मीं or म्यां by me.

Upon all neuter pronouns; as तें it.

Upon the final letter of the gerund and the infinitive; as करणें doing, करूं to do.

Upon the final letter of the verb agreeing with the first personal pronoun, and a neuter word; as मो सोडितों I loose, तें सुटलें It has got loose.

Upon the last letter of a verb agreeing with a second personal pronoun in the plural number; तुम्ही जातां you go.

Upon the present participles in तां, तांना.

When the vowels अ and आ, ओ and वो, ई and यां, ए and ये, and ओ, are interchangeable,

(a) *Initially* अ is preferable to आ; लहान little, to लाहान or लाहन.

(b) ओ is preferable to वो; ओढणें to वोढणें to pull; दरोड़ा to दर्वोड़ा.

(c) ई is *finally* preferable to यो; बाई to बायी a lady.

All monosyllables containing ई or ऊ should be written with long vowels; पीठ flour, मीठ salt, ऊठ arise, ऊ a louse.

But if the ई or ऊ has an Anusvára over it, it should be shortened; as चिंच tamarind, उंट a camel. The imitative particles are written with the short इ or उ; as पुटपुट, किरकिर.

The initial ई or ऊ of any other word than a monosyllable should be short; as शिकणें to learn, भुसकट chaff, गुडघा a knee.

The final ई and ऊ are always long; गढी a fortress, लाडू a cake.

A word ending in a dento-palatal ज does not take य when inflected under the sixth declension; as राजा a king, राजाला and not राज्याला.

च, ज, झ, are pronounced as full palatals in combination with ई. स is often pronounced and written as इा; as स्यासीं or त्याझीं.

The dento-palatals च, ज, झ, &c. are written with a dot (.) before the transverse line at their head; राजा, *rádzá*, a king.

CHAPTER III.

ETYMOLOGY.

GENERAL OBSERVATIONS ON THE CLASSIFICATION AND INFLECTION OF WORDS.

26. Etymology treats of the Classification (जाति, वर्ग), Inflection, (रूप), and Derivation (व्युत्पत्ति) of Words.

27. Words are divided into Eight Classes, according to their signification or uses: viz. Substantive (नाम), Adjective (विशेषण), Pronoun (सर्वनाम), Verb (क्रियापद), Adverb (क्रियाविशेषण), Preposition or Postposition (शब्दयोगी अव्यय), Conjunction (उभयान्वयी अव्यय), and Interjection (केवळप्रयोगी अव्यय).

28. Of these words the first four are inflected, *i. e.*, they are modified to indicate their relation to other words in the sentence, while the last four are generally uninflected. The inflected words are called (सविभक्तिक) *Declinable*, and the uninflected are called (अव्यय or अविभक्तिक) *Particles*.

29. The inflection of a word according to its grammatical Cases is called *Declension* (विभक्तिकार्य), and the inflection of a word according to its Tenses, Moods, &c. is called *Conjugation*, रूप or रूपें चालवणें. Only Verbs are *conjugated*.

30. The inflections of words indicating their *Number* and *Gender* are included both in Declension and Conjugation.

31. *Number* (वचन) is the distinction of objects, as one, or more than one, expressed by a difference in the form of a word.

In Marāṭhí there are two Numbers, the *Singular number* (एकवचन) and the *Plural number* (अनेकवचन). The Singular number denotes only one object, and the Plural number denotes more than one.

Note. In some languages, such as the Sanskrit, Greek, &c. there are three numbers. The third one is the *Dual number* द्विवचन, denoting *two* objects.

32. *Gender* is a difference in words or their inflections to express distinction of *Sex*.

There are three Genders (लिंग): viz. the *Masculine gender*, the *Feminine gender*, and the *Neuter gender*.

When a word has a form, or is construed as a word, expressive of a male being, it is said to be in the *Masculine gender* (पुंल्लिंग).

When a word has a form, or is construed like a word, denoting a female being, it is said to be in the *Feminine gender* (स्त्रीलिंग).

When a word has a form, or is construed like a word, expressing neither a male nor a female, it is said to be in the *Neuter gender* (नपुंसक).

Note. In some languages, such as the Hindí, there are only *two* genders, all words being considered as pertaining to a male or female.

Note. Since only living beings are either male or female, the names or words pertaining to these ought alone to be either masculine or feminine; such is the case in English. It classes all other names or words, denoting objects destitute of life, under the neuter gender; in this respect it differs from Maráṭhí, Sanskrit and its dialects, Latin, Greek, &c., which assign the masculine and feminine gender even to names of things.

CHAPTER IV.
SUBSTANTIVES.

33. A word used as the designation or appellation of a being or thing, existing in fact or thought, is a *Noun*, or a *Noun Substantive*; as घर a house, शहाणपण wisdom.

34. Nouns are *Proper* (विशेष), *Common* (सामान्य), and *Abstract* (भाववाचक).

The name of a particular person or thing is a *Proper Noun*; the name pertaining to *any one* of a class of objects, as well as to the *whole* class, is a *Common Noun*; the name of an attribute of an object, viewed as a distinct entity, is an *Abstract Noun*. A *Concrete Noun* (गुणविशिष्ट) is the name which stands for an object together with its attributes.

I.—Cases of Substantives.

35. *Case* (विभक्ति) is the form of a Substantive by which its relation to the other words in the sentence is indicated.

36. There are seven principal relations indicated by Márathí nouns, by a change of form, and hence there are *seven* Cases in Márathí.

Note. We have, below, recognized Eight Cases, dividing the first Case into the Nominative case and Accusative case.

Note. The Sanskrit grammarians mention Eight cases, but the Sanskrit *Dvitíyá* (Accusative) has not a form in Márathí, distinct either from the *Prathamá* (Nominative) or the *Chaturthí* (Dative). In Prákrit, which is the immediate source of Márathí, there is, however, a distinct form for the Accusative.

37. The seven Cases are thus designated by the Márathí (Sanskrit) grammarians: प्रथमा (or "the first" case), तृतीया (the 3rd), चतुर्थी (the 4th), पंचमी (the 5th), षष्ठी (the 6th), सप्तमी (the 7th), and संबोधन (the Vocative).

38. The *Prathamá* is the unaltered form of the noun, and expresses both the subject and the object of the verb.

When the *Prathamá* expresses the *subject* (कर्त्ता) of the verb, it is called, in this book, the *Nominative Case*; as पंतोजी शिकवितो The master teaches. When it expresses the *object* (कर्म) of the verb, it is called the *Accusative Case*; as मुलगा आंबा खातो The boy eats a mango.

39. The *Tritíyá* usually expresses the *instrument* (करण) of an action; as तो हानानें खातो He eats with the hand. This is called the *Instrumental Case*.

It expresses also *agency*; as त्यानें काम केलें He did the work.

40. The *Chaturthí* expresses principally the *indirect object* (संप्रदान) of the verb, and answers to the question "Unto whom?" or "to or for what?" ब्राह्मणाला गाय दे Give a cow to the Bráhman, ती शाळेंत जायाला रडते She cries to go (or for going) to school. This is called the *Dative Case*.

It expresses, also, the direct object (कर्म); त्यानें रामाला मारिलें He beat Rámá.

41. The *Panchami* expresses the source (अपादान) whence any thing proceeds; मी घरून आलों I came from the house. This is called the *Ablative Case*.

It expresses, also, the relation of *locality*; म्यां दुरून पाहिलें I saw from afar: also, of *Comparison*, तो त्याच्याहून मोठी आहे She is bigger than he.

42. The *Shashthi* expresses the relation (संबंध) of origin, or possession between two nouns; as रामाचें पुस्तक Rámá's book. This is called the *Genitive Case*.

43. The *Saptami* indicates the relation of locality or position (अभिकरण); as त्याच्या डोकीं पागोटें नव्हतें He had not a turban on his head. This is called the *Locative Case*.

44. The *Sambodhana* is used in addressing an object; गड्यानों आपला खेळगडी कृष्ण मथुरेचा राजा झाला Friends, our playmate Krishṇa has become the king of Mathurá. This is called the *Vocative Case*.

45. The inflections which are affixed to the substantives to form the several cases are the following:—

Cases.	Singular.	Plural.
Nominative and Accusative.	Name.	Name.
Instrumental.	एं, नें, शीं.	ईं, हीं, नीं, शीं.
Dative.	ला, स.	ना, ला, स.
Ablative.	ऊन, हून.	ऊन, हून.
Genitive.	चा *m.* ची *f.* चें *n.*	चा *m.* ची *f.* चें *n.*
Locative.	आं, ई	आं, ई
Vocative.	The *crude* form.	नों

46. The following prepositions are employed by some grammarians in the place of the above case-endings:—

(18)

Inst. करून, करवीं, कडून, जवळून, द्वारें, मुळें.
Dat. प्रत, जवळ, लागोनीं, कारणें, करितां, साठीं, अर्थ, अर्थीं, रतव.
Abl. कडून, करून, पासून, पेक्षां, वरून.
Gen. संबंधी.
Loc. आंत, कडे, ठायीं, मध्यें, विषयीं.
Voc. अरे, रे, अगा, गा, हे, अजि Mas. Sing. } अहो, अजी M. F. Plu.
अगे, गे, अगो Fem. Sing.

Note. The Particles of the Vocative case are placed before the noun; as अरे राजा O king.

Note. Some of the postpositions are preferred by natives to the true case-ending. आंत is usually employed to express the locative relation, and, indeed, some words do not take the true case-endings to express that relation. Hence we have occasionally used आंत *in* to make up the Locative case.

Note. Sometimes, a noun takes both its case-ending and a postposition to express a case-relation, as, शस्त्रेंकरून By means of a weapon, शस्त्रें + करून or कडून, denoting simple instrumentality. The case-ending ऍ is usually used in this way.

Note. Sometimes, it takes two case-endings at the same time; त्याच्यानें बोलवलें नाहीं He could not speak = त्याचा + नें, denoting agency.

Note. In poetry, chiefly, the noun, without either its case-endings or postpositions, is used to indicate a case-relation. The word, then, assumes what is called the सामान्यरूप or crude form, as—

म्हणोनि तुमच्याच मी स्मरतसें सदा पावला,

It is therefore that I worship (remember) at your feet; पावला = पावलाला To feet. So also in the proverb बोले लेकी लागे सुने ¡The mother-in-law punishes a daughter-in-law by scolding her own daughter.

Note. The case-endings and the postpositions, sometimes, alter their forms in poetry. Thus,

यशोदेसी त्या भासती तत्समाना ह्यावाच्या जशा पूतळ्या वर्तमाना. *Wáman.*

II. Numbers of Substantives.

47. The Maráthí substantives take a plural form either to denote the idea of plurality, or of civility; thus साठे, the plural of साठ्या, which is a surname, may denote either that there are many persons who have the surname of Sáthe, or that only one man is spoken of with respect.

48. The names of materials are generally used in the singular; पाणी water, गहूं wheat, &c.

49. Some nouns have not a distinct form for the plural; बाप a father, or fathers.

(1) All masculine substantives, with the exception of those ending in आ, are of this class; as हात a hand, or hands.

(2) Feminine nouns ending in आ, इ, उ; as माता a mother, or mothers.

50. Some nouns have only a plural form; as मुस्क्या the arms as tied behind the back.

51. Some nouns have both a plural and a collective form; as पैसा, money, is singular in form, but denote one or many; पैसे is the plural form.

52. Some nouns have two singular forms, but one plural form; as केळ or केळें a plantain, केळीं plantains; नारळ or नारळी a cocoanut tree, नारळी cocoanut trees, &c.

53. Some nouns change their forms in the plural.

(1) Masculine nouns ending in आ change their final vowel to ए; thus,

Singular.	Plural.
आंबा A mango.	आंबे Mangoes.
भाट्या A Bhátyá.	भाट्ये Bhatyás.

Note. Proper nouns do not take a plural form; as रामा, Rámá, singular & plural.

(20).

(2) Feminine nouns in अ change the अ either to आ or ई, and sometimes to both; thus,

खूण A sign.	खुणा Signs.
भिंत A wall.	भिंती Walls.
तरवार A sword.	तरवारा or -वारी Swords.

Note. Nouns of the Third Declension change the भ to आ, and those of the Fourth Declension to ई, and rarely to आ.

(3) Feminine nouns in ई change the ई to या; as काठी a stick, काठ्या sticks.

Note. Words ending in a simple ई form their plural in two ways; आई a mother, आई or आया plural.

Note. Words of Sanskrit and other foreign origin are exceptions; as दासी (S.) a handmaiden, or handmaidens; मस्करी (H.) a jest, or jests.

Note. If words ending in ई drop the ई, their plural retains its first form; as सू (सुई) a needle, सुया needles.

(4) Feminine nouns in ऊ change the ऊ to वा or अवा; सासू a mother-in-law, सासवा or सासवा mothers-in-law.

Note. Sanskrit and other foreign words do not follow this rule; as बाजू (H.) a side, sing. and plur.

(5) Feminine nouns in ओ change the final vowel to आ; as बायको a woman, बायका women.

(6) Neuter nouns in अ, ई and ऊ assume the final एं:—

Singular.	Plural.
घर A house.	घरें Houses.
मोती A pearl.	मोत्यें Pearls.
वासरूं A calf.	वासरें Calves.

Note. Neuter nouns ending in ऊं of the Fifth Declension, only, change the ऊं to एं, but the nouns in ऊं that fall under the Sixth Declension, change it to वें or अवें; as तारूं a ship, तारवें or तावें ships.

(7). Neuter nouns ending in एं take the final ईं; as तळें a tank, तळीं tanks.

54. The following table will show at one glance which nouns are inflected, and which not, in the plural :—

Singular Terminations.			Plural.	Terminations.	
M.	F.	N.	M.	F.	N.
अ			अ	आ, ई	एं
आ			ए	आ	
इ			इ	इ	इ
ई			ई	या	ये
उ			उ	उ	उ
ऊ			ऊ	वा or भवा	एं, वें or अवें ई
ए				या	
ऐ				आ	
ओ			ओ	वा	
औ			औ		

III. The Genders of Substantives.

55. The genders of Maráṭhí nouns, like those of the Sanskrit, Latin, &c., cannot be always ascertained, either by their form, or their signification.

The student must acquire a knowledge of them by the help of a dictionary, or intercourse with natives.

Maráṭhí grammarians have, however, attempted to lay down rules to determine the genders, and obtained considerable success. The rules are based on (1) the *form* of words, and (2) their *signification*.

I. *Rules for Determining the Gender of Nouns by their Forms.*

56. (I). Pure Maráṭhí and Hindusthání words in आ are generally masculine; as पैका money, अंगठा a thumb.

(2) Sanskrit nouns ending in आ are feminine; as कथा a tale.

(3) Nouns in ई are generally feminine.

Note. Sanskrit words are exceptions; as संधि an opportunity, m. f.; ध्वनि a voice, m. f.; अग्नि fire, m.; पक्षी a bird, m.; माणिक a jewel, m.

(4) Nouns ending in इ, उ. and ए are neuter; *exc.* गहूं wheat, m.

(5) Nouns in ए and ऐ are feminine; as सवे a habit, सै a signature.

(6) Nouns in ओ are usually feminine; as बायको a woman.

Exc. The following nouns, besides appellations of males, are masculine; डाहो sensation of burning; मोहो a bee's nest, m. n.; टाहो a moaning, लाहो covetousness.

(7) Compound nouns have generally the same gender as the last member of the compound; as अंगवस्त्र a garment, n., because वस्त्र is neuter; करपटाण = करपट + घाण, smell of singed food, f., घाण being feminine.

(8) Abstract nouns (excepting those ending in ता, f., and पणा, m.) are all neuter; as सौंदर्य beauty, चांगुलपण goodness.

II. *Rules for Determining the Genders of Nouns by Signification.*

57. (1) Names of living beings are, according to the sex, either masculine or feminine; मुलगा a boy, m.; मुलगी a girl, f.

Note. Some nouns are used in more than one gender; as माणूस a person, m. n. पोर, मूल a child, m. f. n.

Note. Diminutives ending in a neuter termination are of the neuter gender; गायरूं a small cow.

Note. Many names of animals have a standing form common to animals of both sexes; कोल्हा is a male jackal; or a jackal generally, either male or female.

(2) Names of mountains, seas, winds, rain, clouds, are masculine; समुद्र a sea, डोंगर a mountain, पाऊस rain, &c.

Note. हवा air, f.; वरसात rain, f.; ढग a cloud, m.; n.; अभ्र a cloud, n.; आकाश the sky, n., &c.

(3) Names of time and its divisions, as days, months, years, &c., and the names of the planets, are masculine.

Note. Exc. When वेळ time denotes a particular time, it is feminine; as त्याची मरणाची वेळ आली His time of death has arrived: but otherwise, it is masculine; as किती वेळ झाला what time is it? पृथ्वी the earth, and lunar days or तिथि, such as प्रतिपदा the first lunar day, &c., are feminine. तारा a star, is both masculine and feminine.

(4) Names of rivers are feminine; गोदावरी the Godávarí.

Note. Exc. Those called Nadas and Upanadas, such as सिंधु the Indus, &c., are masculine.

(5) Names of the points of the compass, as पूर्व the east, वायवी the north-west, &c., are feminine.

(6) Names of metals are neuter; सोनें gold, जस्त zinc.

Note. Exc. पितळ brass, f. n.

(7) Names of water and its formations are neuter; as पाणी water, तेलवणी oil and water; so also the names of oil, and of milk and its products (excepting nouns in आ, which are masculine, and सहा or साय, cream, which is feminine); as एरंडेल castor oil, लोणी butter, &c.

Note. Imperfect as these rules are, they will be found very useful by the student of Maráthí. Very simple but most practical rules on the determination of the gender *of a noun occurring in a reading lesson* are the following:—

(*a*) Find out the verb which agrees with the noun, and the personal endings of the verb would denote the gender, as रामा लिहितो Rámá writes.

(*b*) An adjective or an adverb ending in आ, ई, or एं, and referring to the noun, would indicate its gender; पांढरा दांत A white tooth; सखू चांगली नाचेल Sakhú will dance well.

(*c*) A pronoun pertaining to the noun would indicate its gender by its form; as घर जें The house which.

58. Some substantives receive different terminations according as they designate male or female beings.

59. (1) Masculine nouns ending in आ have a feminine termination in ई, and a neuter termination in एं; as मुलगा a boy, मुलगी a girl, मुलगें a child.

☞ *Note.* These terminations, viz. आ m., ई f., and एं n., together with their plurals, ए m., या f., and ईं n., are the *principal* gender terminations in Maráthí; and *the only gender terminations which adjectives, adverbs, most verbal forms, and most pronouns assume.*

(2) Masculine nouns ending in अ assume the feminine termination ई or ईण; as हरण a deer, हरणी f.; वाघ a tiger, वाघीण a tigress.

Note. The masculine form, sometimes, serves for the neuter; as हरण m. n. Pure Sanskrit words take ई in the feminine; as दास a servant, दासी f.; ब्राह्मण A Bráhman, ब्राह्मणी f.

(3) Masculine nouns ending in ई and उ have a feminine form in ईण; as हत्ती an elephant, हत्तीण f.; परभू A Parbhú, परभीण f.

60. Some nouns have more than one neuter termination; as, बकरा a goat, बकरी f., बकरें or बकरूं n. Sometimes they have a distinct neuter word, besides that derived from the root; as घोडा a horse, घोडी f., घोडें or शिंगरूं n.; बकरा a goat, बकरी f., बकरें or करडूं n.

Note. Of these forms, those in एं denote the *species generally*, without reference to its sex, or *an individual in contempt; as* बकरें A goat,—spoken revilingly, or without any reference to its sex; बकरूं or करडूं a young goat only.

61. Some substantives, denoting *inanimate* objects, assume gender terminations; गाडा a cart, m., गाडी f., गाडें n.

Note. When a feminine noun ending in ई takes the masculine termination आ, it signifies a large, clumsy object, and its neuter form in एं denotes that the object is spoken revilingly; thus गाडा a cart, गाडी a carriage; गाडें a cart or carriage, spoken revilingly; भाकरी a cake of bread, भाकरा a huge cake of bread.

Note. Another peculiarity of the Maráthí language is noticed in दोरा m. a thread, दोरी a rope, दोर a cable.

62. The following masculine words have corresponding *distinct* feminine words:—

Masculine.	Feminine.
इंट A camel.	साड A she-camel.
काळवीट A deer.	हरणी A hind.
गवळी A milkman.	गवळण A milkwoman.
दीर A brother-in-law.	जाऊ A sister-in-law.
पुरुष A man.	बायकी A woman.
नवरा A husband.	बायकी A wife.
बाप A father.	आई A mother.
बैल An ox.	गाई A cow.
बोकड A he-goat.	शेळी A she-goat, करडूं n.
बोका A he-cat.	मांजर A she-cat, मांजरूं n.
भाऊ A brother.	बहीण A sister.
मावळा An uncle.	मावळण An aunt.
मोर A peacock.	लांडोर A peahen.
रेडा A he-buffalo.	म्हैस A she-buffalo.
राजा A king.	राणी A queen.
सासरा A father-in-law.	सासू A mother-in-law.

CHAPTER V.
DECLENSION OF SUBSTANTIVES.

63. Declension is a change of termination in substantives, to express the different relations in which they stand to other words in the same sentence; as बाप a father, बापाचें घर, a father's house.

64. Before the terminations, which indicate the various relations, are affixed to the substantive, it undergoes a change of form. The form which it thus assumes is called the सामान्यरूप or *crude form*. Thus, घर a house becomes घरा before the genitive termination ना is joined to it—घराना of a house.

65. Maráṭhí substantives assume, in all, *six* different forms before the case terminations, or, in other words, have six different crude forms, and hence there are Six Declensions विभक्तिप्रकार. Each of these declensions has a peculiar termination *in the dative singular*; thus,

Declensions.	I.	II.	III.	IV.	V.	VI.
Terminations of the Dative Singular.	The same as the Nominative Case.	Long vowel.	ए	ई	आ	या or वा यें or वें

Nominative Terminations.

OBSERVATIONS.

अ
{
(1) All masculine and neuter nouns in अ are of the 2nd declension.

(2) All feminines in अ are either of the 3rd or of the 4th declension.
}

आ
{
(3) All masculine nouns (excepting proper nouns and names of respect) ending in आ are of the 6th declension.

(4) All feminine nouns terminating in आ (excepting names of respect, and proper names) are of the 3rd declension.
}

ई
{
(5) All masculine nouns in ई (excepting proper names, names of respect, and a few such words as हत्ती, &c.) are of the 6th declension.

(6) All feminine nouns in ई (excepting स्त्री a woman, and one or two more words) are of the 1st declension.
}

ऊ
{
(7) Masculine nouns in ऊ chiefly belong to the 6th declension. A few may belong to the 1st and 5th.

(8) All feminine nouns in ऊ belong to the 1st declension. A few of them may, also, belong to the 6th.

(9) Neuter nouns in ऊ may belong either to the 5th or the 6th declension.
}

इ and उ } (10) All nouns ending in short इ and उ are of the 2nd declension.

ए (11) Neuter nouns ending in ए are of the 6th declension.

Miscellaneous. } (12) Masculine and feminine nouns terminating in ए, ऐ, ओ, and औ are of the 1st declension.

66. The following is an example of a substantive declined with all the case-endings, specified in the 45th section :—

Singular.

Nom.	घर A house.
Acc.	घर A house.
Inst.	घरानें, घरें, घराशीं, or सीं By a house.
Dat.	घरा, घरास, घराला To a house.
Abl.	घराहून, घरहून From a house.
Gen.	घराचा m. -ची f. -चें n. घराने m. -च्या f. -चीं n. } Of a house.
Loc.	घरी, घरीं In or at a house.
Voc.	घरा O house.

Plural.

Nom.	घरें Houses.
Acc.	घरें Houses.
Inst.	घरानीं, घराहीं, घराशीं, or-सीं By or with houses.
Dat.	घरास, घराला, घराना To houses.
Abl.	घराहून From houses.
Gen.	घराचा m. -ची f. -चें n. घराचे m. -च्या f. -चीं n. } Of houses.
Loc.	घरीं At or in houses.
Voc.	घरानों O houses.

Note 1. The instrumental in ए is seldom used, except with the postposition करुन or कडून By or with, as शस्त्रेंकरुन By means of a weapon.

2. According to the principles of combination specified in Sec. 24, the case-endings beginning with a vowel displace the final vowel of the crude form; as घरा + ए = घरें By a house; घरा + ऊन = घरून From a house; घरा + ईं = घरीं In a house; घरा + आ = घरा In a house.

3. Since the locative endings आं and ईं are rarely used, we have supplied their place by using the postposition आंत in.

First Declension.

(पहिला विभक्तिप्रकार.)

67. In this declension the nominative singular and the crude form are identical; as गाडी a carriage, गाडीला to a carriage. The following words are included under it:—

(1) The letters of the Alphabet; as क ka, ख kha, &c. Thus क ka, कला to a ka.

(2) All proper names and names of respect, both of males and females; as रामा Rámá, रामाला to Rámá; दादा a brother, दादाला to a brother; रमा Ramá (f.), रमाला to Ramá.

(3) All nouns ending in ए and ओ; as सवे a habit, सवेला to a habit; बायको a woman, बायकोला to a woman.

Note. Nouns ending in ऐ and औ are variously spelt; thus, तिवे, तिवई, or तिवय a tripod; पौ, पऊ, or पव, a mark upon a die. They are declined according to their final vowel; thus तिवेला, तिवईला (1st decl.), or तिवयेला (3rd decl.); पौला, पऊला (1st decl.), or पवाला (2nd decl.)

(4) All masculine nouns ending in ऊ, except those specified under the fifth and sixth declensions; as चाकू a pen-knife, चाकूला to a pen-knife.

(5) Feminine nouns in ई and ऊ, excepting those specified under the sixth declension; गाडी a carriage, गाडीला to a carriage; खडू f., chalk, खडूला to chalk.

(6) Abstract nouns in पणा and verbal nouns in नारा; as चांगुलपणा goodness, चांगुलपणाला to goodness; बोलणारा a speaker, बोलणाराला to a speaker.

(7) The following neuter nouns in उं :—

अवाळूं, आगरूं, उडाणूं, उवाळूं, खट्टूं, चांटूं, छाछूं, जानूं, टाटूं, पाचेरूं, फार्फूं, राजाळूं, हांहुं, हुंचूं.

Examples.

बाबा m. A father.

	Singular.	Plural.
Nom.	बाबा	बाबा
Acc.	बाबा	बाबा
Inst.	बाबानें-शीं	बाबानीं-शीं
Dat.	बाबाला-स	बाबांला-ना-स
Abl.	बाबाहून	बाबाहून
Gen.	बाबाचा-ची-चें	बाबांचा-ची-चें
Loc.	बाबांत	बाबांत
Voc.	बाबा	बाबानों

सासू f. A mother-in-law.

	Singular.	Plural.
Nom.	सासू	सासवा.
Acc.	सासू	सासवा.
Inst.	सासूनें	सासवानीं
Dat.	सासूला	सासवाला
Abl.	सासूहून	सासवाहून.
Gen.	सासूचा-ची-चें	सासवाचा-ची-चें
Loc.	सासूंत	सासवांत.
Voc.	सासू	सासवानीं

गाडी f. A carriage.

	Singular.	Plural.
Nom.	गाडी	गाड्या
Acc.	गाडी	गाड्या
Inst.	गाडीनें	गाड्यानीं
Dat.	गाडीला	गाड्याला
Abl.	गाडीहून	गाड्याहून
Gen.	गाडीचा	गाड्याचा
Loc.	गाडींत	गाड्यांत
Voc.	गाडी	गाड्यानीं

बायको f. A woman.

	Singular.	Plural.
Nom.	बायको	बायका
Acc.	बायको	बायका
Inst.	बायकोनें	बायकानीं
Dat.	बायकोला	बायकाला
Abl.	बायकोहून	बायकाहून
Gen.	बायकोचा-ची-चें	बायकांचा-ची-चें
Loc.	बायकोंत	बायकांत
Voc.	बायको	बायकानीं

गेरू m. A red chalk.

	Singular.	Plural.
Nom.	गेरू	गेरू
Acc.	गेरू	गेरू
Inst.	गेरूनें	गेरूनीं.
Dat.	गेरूला	गेरूंला.
Abl.	गेरूहून	गेरूंहून.
Gen.	गेरूचा-ची-चें	गेरूंचा-ची-चें.
Loc.	गेरूंत	गेरूंत.
Voc.	गेरू	गेरूनों.

हत्ती m. An elephant.

	Singular.	Plural.
Nom.	हत्ती	हत्ती
Acc.	हत्ती	हत्ती
Inst.	हत्तीनें	हत्तींनीं
Dat.	हत्तीला	हत्तींला
Abl.	हत्तीहून	हत्तींहून.
Gen.	हत्तीचा-ची-चें	हत्तींचा-ची-चें
Loc.	हत्तींत	हत्तींत.
Voc.	हत्ती	हत्तींनों.

Second Declension.

68. The substantives of this declension make their crude form by *lengthening* the final vowel of the nominative singular; as बाप a father, बापाला to a father.

Under this declension are included the following substantives:—

(1) Masculine and neuter nouns ending in अ; चीक m. pith, चिकाला to the pith; घर n. a house, घराला to a house.

(2) All nouns ending in short इ and उ; कवि m. a poet, कवीला to a poet; रुचि f. taste, रुचीला to taste; धातु m. a metal, धातूला to a metal; मधु n. honey, मधूला to honey; धेनु f. a cow, धेनूला to a cow.

EXAMPLES.

देव A god.

	Singular.	Plural.
Nom.	देव	देव
Acc.	देव	देव
Inst.	देवानें	देवानीं
Dat.	देवाला	देवांला
Abl.	देवाहून	देवांहून
Gen.	देवाचा-ची-चें	देवांचा-ची-चें.
Loc.	देवांत	देवांत
Voc.	देव or देवा	देवांनों

कवि m. A poet.

	Singular.	Plural.
Nom.	कवि	कवि
Acc.	कवि	कवि
Inst.	कवीनें	कवींनीं
Dat.	कवीला	कवींला
Abl.	कवीहून	कवींहून
Gen.	कवीचा-ची-चें	कवींचा-ची-चें
Loc.	कवींत	कवींत
Voc.	कवी	कवींनों

मधु n. Honey.

	Singular.	Plural.
Nom.	मधु	मधु
Acc.	मधु	मधु
Inst.	मधूनें	मधूंनीं
Dat.	मधूला	मधूंला
Abl.	मधूहून	मधूंहून
Gen.	मधूचा-ची-चें	मधूंचा-ची-चें
Loc.	मधूंत	मधूंत
Voc.	मधू	मधूंनों

Third Declension.

69. The third declension changes the terminating vowel of the nominative case to ए in the crude form; जीभ a tongue, जिभेला to a tongue.

This declension comprises the following nouns:—

(1) All feminine nouns derived from the Sanskrit and ending in आ; as माता a mother, मातेला to a mother.

Note. Proper nouns, and Sanskrit nouns of rare use in Marāthí, are of the 1st declension; as रमा Ramá (a name of a girl), रमाला to Ramá; चंद्रमा the moon, चंद्रमाला to the moon, &c.

(2) All feminine nouns ending in अ, and specified in the following list:—

अटक	आब	एकवेळ	कास	खडव	खेव
अडक	आवोस	एळ	काळवेळ	खडीसाखर	गजक
अडवाट	इरजीक	एरीण	काळीधार	खरडोंग	गंजीफ
अडवेळ	इट	ओली खरूज	किलच	खरूज	गप
अंतरखुण	इंद	कड	किलीच	खाक	गरज
अंबुरकी चिंच	उखळबेरीज	कणऊब	किल्स	खाट	गरुडपान
अलंग	उणोव	कणीक	कुमक	खारीक	गुंज
अवेळ	उतरती वेळ	कंवर or कमर	कुळीक	खीज	गुंफ
अहेव	उतारपेंठ	करप	कैद	खूण	गुराव
अळवीण	उतारवेळ	कव	कोईल	खुप	गुलेमख
आउंज	उपारपेठ	कांच	कोईळ	खेंप	गोंदे
आन	ऊप	कांव	गच	खेग	गोरखचिंच

(32)

घउमाळ	टीक	तेरीख	परतवेळ	भांग	मोहोम	लाभवेळ	
घोडशीर	टीच	तेरोज	पर्पेंठ	भाचेसून	मौज	लाऊन	
घोडेवाट	टीप	तोंडबाग	पश्चिम	भाज	म्हसक	लंव	
चढती वेळ	डाक	तोफ	पहाट	भाड	रकम	लाळ	
चपटालाख	डाग	दरज	पाच	भाष	रतनगुंज	लीख	
चपडालाख	डेग	दवणशीर	पाणड्रोंग	भोस	रयत	लीड	
चपडास	डेंग	दवणोपुनव	पाणसळ	भिक्राळ	राख	लोखंडीकांव	
चाईन	डांग	दाद	पायवाट	भिक्राळ	राखूळ	लोंग	
चार	डेंग	दाणालाख	पिठीसाखर	भीक्	रांग	वज्रटीक	
चाम्हरीमोट	ढेलच	दाणासाखर	पीण	भीड	राड	वडुनव	
चिंच	ढोणशीर	दीपमाळ	पुनव	भूक	राडखाड	वदणूक	
चितंग	तज	दुरव	पुन्येव	भूज	राडमुंड	वधूमाय	
चिवार	तजवीज	दुशाख	पूर्व	भोंवंड	रातनवाव	वत्तेणूक	
चीज	तन	धर्मनाव	पेठ	भोवळ	रानघोळ	वस्न	
चोढ or ड	तनाव	धर्मव्रट	पैज	मध	रानवाट	वहाण	
चीप	तरफ	ध्रुव	फातमा	मनभूक	रिकामवेळ	वाट	
चोर	तलफ	भूळवाफ	फाम	मरतबांझ	रीघ	वाफ	
चील	तवसाळ	थोंडशीर	फिरंग	मसक	रोझ	वाभळ	
चुणूक	तसर	धोप	फुंक	मसूर	रोप	वांव	
चेंगडालाख	तखरीफ	नजर	फौज	महमाय	रोस	विलायन	
चोरवाट	तहान	नजरपारख	व	माठ	रेघ	बीज	
जंजीर	तळवाट	नणंद	बग	मांडणूक	रेंव	बोट	
जट	तक्षोम	नथ	बंदरवाट	मान	रेंव	बोड	
जांग	ताऊज	नमाज	बाग	माद	रेवड	बोळ	
जाग	तागलवाट	नरद	बाज	मादवान	रोंथ	वेंग	
जाप	ताज	नागदवण	बाजारबैठक्	मादूस	लव	वेण	
जाणीव	ताजोम	नातसून	बांधवाट	मान	लवंग	वेळ	
जिलह or ढहे	तान	नार्व्लीपुनव	वाम	मानणूक	लवणशाक	वेळ अवेळ	
जीभ	तान्ह	नालमेख	वाळभूक	माय	लशीखरूज	शाक or ग्र	
जेवणवेळ	ताब	नाव	बोज	माव	लशुन	शाल	
झउप	तार	नोज	बोद	माळ	लांक	शाळ	
झीज	तारीख	नीद	बुरासाखर	मिळतोवस्त	लाख	शिंक	
झूम	तालीम	नेणीव	बुज	मुसळधार	लांच	शिंगकं	
झूर	तिउक	पईज	बेत	मेंग	लाज	शिंप	
झांप	तिडीक	पंचधार	बाद	मोच	लाट	शिलक	
टांग	तीज	पडजीभ	बॉंब	मोट	लाण	शिव	
टिंच	तीट	पडसाळ	भाउबीज	मोहनमान	लात	शुभवेळ	
टिवारीव	तूळ	पत्राज or स	भाक	मोहोर	लानाउ	शोंक	

(33)

रोज	सकाळ	सवन	साजवेळ	सिंक	सोंड	हरमूज
रोंच	सडक	सहाण	साड	सिकल	सोनकाव	होतीवस्तन.
रोंद	सदर	साखर	साण	सींव	हाक	
रोंर	समोध	साखरझोंप	साद	सूज	हाव	
रोंस	सव	साज or झ	साव	सून	हरऊभूज	

EXAMPLES.

माता A mother.

	Singular.	Plural.
Nom.	माता	माता
Acc.	माता	माता
Inst.	मातेनें	मातांनीं
Dat.	मातेला	मातांला
Abl.	मातेहून	मातांहून
Gen.	मातेचा-ची-चें	मातांचा-ची-चें
Loc.	मातेंत	मातांत
Voc.	माते	मातांनों

चिंच A tamarind.

	Singular.	Plural.
Nom.	चिंच	चिंचा
Acc.	चिंच	चिंचा
Inst.	चिंचेनें	चिंचांनीं
Dat.	चिंचेला	चिंचांला
Abl.	चिंचेहून	चिंचांहून
Gen.	चिंचेचा-ची-चें	चिंचांचा-ची-चें
Loc.	चिंचेंत	चिंचांत
Voc.	चिंचे	चिंचांनों

Fourth Declension.

70. In the fourth declension, the crude form changes the terminating vowel of the nominative case to ई; as आग fire, आगीला to the fire.

This declension includes the following nouns:—

(1) Persian and Arabic words, ending in त, द, न; as दौत an inkstand, दौतीला to an inkstand; उमेद confidence, उमेदीला to confidence: In short, all the feminine words ending in अ that are not *included in the list of words of the third declension.*

5 m a

Examples.

गोष्ट A word or matter.

	Singular.	Plural.
Nom.	गोष्ट	गोष्टी
Acc.	गोष्ट	गोष्टी
Inst.	गोष्टीनें	गोष्टींनीं
Dat.	गोष्टीला	गोष्टींला
Abl.	गोष्टीहून	गोष्टींहून
Gen.	गोष्टी चा-ची-चें	गोष्टी चा-ची-चें
Loc.	गोष्टींत	गोष्टींत
Voc.	गोष्ट	गोष्टींनों

Fifth Declension.

71. The fifth declension changes the terminating vowel of the nominative case to आ, in order to make up the crude form; as वाटसरू a traveller, वाटसराला to a traveller.

This includes the following nouns :—

Masculine and neuter substantives ending in उ and ऊ; as यात्रेकरू m. a pilgrim, यात्रेकराला to a pilgrim; वांसरूं a calf, वांसराला to a calf.

Note. There are only about two or three masculine nouns ending in ऊ, such as परभू a caste, वाटसरू a traveller, यात्रेकरू a pilgrim, &c., which are of this declension, the rest being of the first and sixth declensions. Even these two or three masculine words are declinable as words of the first declension.

Note. The following neuter nouns belong to this declension, and some of them also to the first :—

आगरूं	A particular eruption.	फाळकूं	A part of a plough.
किरडूं	A reptile.	मेंढरूं	A sheep.
गुरूं	Horned cattle.	रताळूं	A sweet potato.
टिपरूं	A drumstick.	रेडकूं	A buffalo-calf.
निंबूं	A lime.	वांसरूं	A calf.
पाखरूं	A bird.	शोरडूं	A goat.
पिलूं	A cub.	सुकाणूं	A helm.

—in fact all diminutives ending in रूं and डूं.

EXAMPLES.

तट्टूं n. A pony.

	Singular.	Plural.
Nom.	तट्टूं	तट्टें
Acc.	तट्टूं	तट्टें
Inst.	तट्टानें	तट्टानीं
Dat.	तट्टाला	तट्टांला
Abl.	तट्टाहून	तट्टांहून
Gen.	तट्टाचा-ची-चें	तट्टांचा-ची-चें
Loc.	तट्टांत	तट्टांत
Voc.	तट्टा	तट्टानों

वाटसरू m. A traveller.

	Singular.	Plural.
Nom.	वाटसरू	वाटसरू
Acc.	वाटसरू	वाटसरू
Inst.	वाटसरानें	वाटसरानों
Dat.	वाटसराला	वाटसरांला
Abl.	वाटसराहून	वाटसरांहून
Gen.	वाटसराचा-ची-चें	वाटसरांचा-ची-चें
Loc.	वाटसरांत	वाटसरांत
Voc.	वाटसरा	वाटसरांनों

Sixth Declension.

72. In this declension the crude form changes the final vowel of the nominative singular, *first*, to the semivowel य or व, and *then*, if the substantive be *feminine*, assumes the terminating vowel of the third declension, but, if the substantive be either *masculine* or *neuter*, assumes the terminating vowel of the fifth declension; as सासरा m. a father-in-law, सासन्याला to a father-in-law; सासू f. a mother-in-law, सासवेला or सासवेला to a mother-in-law; मोतीं n. a pearl, मोत्याला to a pearl.

Note. सासरा = सासन्य + आ (5th decl.) = सासन्याला दारू = दारव + ए (3rd decl.) = दारवेला.

This declension includes the following nouns :—

(1) All the neuter nouns that end in ई and ए; मोतीं a pearl, मोत्याला to a pearl; तळें a tank, नळ्याला to a tank.

(2) All nouns in आ, ई, उ and ऊ that do not fall under the first, third, or fifth declension.

Note. (a) All masculine nouns in आ, excepting proper names, and names of respect, belong to this declension; as आत्मा a spirit, आत्म्याला to a spirit; पाटा a grindstone, पाट्याला to a grindstone.

(b) All masculine nouns in ई; as माळी a gardener, माळ्याला to a gardener.

Exc. The only exceptions are those few nouns specified under the first declension; as हत्ती an elephant, हत्तीला to an elephant, &c.

(c) The following masculine nouns in ऊ :—

Exc. Those marked with an asterisk are, also, of the first declension.

	गहूं Wheat.		पू Pus.	*	विंचू A scorpion.
*	गू Fæces.		भाऊ A brother.	*	वेळू A bamboo.
*	चाटू A ladle.		माडू A weapon.		साकू A bridge.
*	नारू Guinea-worm.		रू Cotton.		साडू a brother-in-law.
*	पणतू A great-grandson.		लाडू A sweet cake.		

(d) Monosyllabic feminine nouns ending in ई; स्त्री a woman, स्त्रियेला to a woman.

(e) The following feminine nouns in ऊ belong to this declension, and all the rest to the first; those marked with an asterisk belong, also, to the 1st declension :—

भाऊ	A woman.	पिसू	A flea.
ऊ	A louse.	वेळू	A coil of rope.
जळू	A leech.	बाजू	A side.
जाऊ	A husband's brother's wife.	भालू	A bear.
टाळू	The palate.	वाळू	Sand.
ताळू	The fore part of the head.	सासू	A mother-in-law.
दारू	Spirits.	सू	A needle.

(f) The following neuter nouns in ऊ belong to this declension :—

असूं	A tear.	जूं	A yoke.	बोळूं	Sauce.
अळूं	A vegetable.	तरूं	A ship.	फासूं	A branch of a river.
कुंकूं	A powder.	थरूं	A haft.	वेळूं	A boil.
कुसूं	A town wall.	हूं	A scar.		
गळूं	A boil.	वसूं	An iron ring.		

(g) The following words are of *three* declensions, the first, fifth, and sixth :—

M.	नातू	A grandson.	N.	असूं	A tear.
,,	विंचू	A scorpion.	,,	अळूं	A vegetable.
,,	वेळू	A bamboo.	,,	कुंकूं	A powder.
,,	शाळू	Javári.	,,	कुसूं	A town wall.

Examples.

मिरीं n. Pepper.

	Singular.	Plural.
Nom.	मिरीं	मिर्‍यें
Acc.	मिरीं	मिर्‍यें
Inst.	मिर्‍यानें	मिर्‍यानीं
Dat.	मिर्‍याला	मिर्‍याला
Abl.	मिर्‍याहून	मिर्‍याहून
Gen.	मिर्‍याचा	मिर्‍याचा
Loc.	मिर्‍यांत	मिर्‍यांत
Voc.	मिरीं	मिर्‍यानों

माळी A gardener.

	Singular.	Plural.
Nom.	माळी	माळी
Acc.	माळी	माळी
Inst.	माळ्यानें	माळ्यानीं
Dat.	माळ्याला	माळ्याला
Abl.	माळ्याहून	माळ्याहून
Gen.	माळ्याचा-ची-चें	माळ्याचा-ची-चें
Loc.	माळ्यांत	माळ्यांत
Voc.	माळ्या	माळ्यानों

भाऊ m. A brother.

	Singular.	Plural.
Nom.	भाऊ	भाऊ
Acc.	भाऊ	भाऊ
Inst.	भावानें	भावानीं
Dat.	भावाला	भावाला
Abl.	भावाहून	भावाहून
Gen.	भावाचा-ची चें	भावाचा-ची-चें
Loc.	भावांत	भावांत
Voc.	भावा	भावानों

लाडू m. A cake.

	Singular.	Plural.
Nom.	लाडू	लाडू
Acc.	लाडू	लाडू
Instr.	लाडवानें	लाडवानों
Dat.	लाडवाला	लाडवाला
Abl.	लाडवाहून	लाडवाहून
Gen.	लाडवाचा-ची-चें	लाडवाचा-ची-चें
Loc.	लाडवांत	लाडवांत
Voc.	लाडवा	लाडवानों

स्त्री A woman.

	Singular.	Plural.
Nom.	स्त्रि	स्त्रिया
Acc.	स्त्रि	स्त्रिया
Inst.	स्त्रियेनें	स्त्रियानीं
Dat.	स्त्रियेला	स्त्रियाला
Abl.	स्त्रियेहून	स्त्रियाहून
Gen.	स्त्रियेचा-ची-चें	स्त्रियाचा-ची-चें
Loc.	स्त्रियेंत	स्त्रियांत
Voc.	स्त्रिये	स्त्रियानों

ऊ A louse.

	Singular.	Plural.
Nom.	ऊ	उवा
Acc.	ऊ	उवा
Inst.	उवेनें	उवानीं
Dat.	उवेला	उवाला
Abl.	उवेहून	उवाहून
Gen.	उवेचा-ची-चें	उवाचा-ची-चें
Loc.	उवेंत	उवांत
Voc.	उवे	उवानों

73. The following table combines the particulars given in Section 66, and those mentioned under the several declensions. If but the gender of a noun is known, the student can determine with facility its plural and crude form.

DECLENSION.	I.			II.			III.	IV.	V.		VI.		
Terminations of the Dative Singular.	The same as Nominative Singular.			The terminating Vowel of the Nominative Singular lengthened.			ए	ई	आ		या or वा	ये or वे	या or वा
Genders of Nouns.	M.	F.	N.	M.	F.	N.	F.	F.	M.	N.	M.	F.	N.
Terminating Vowels of the Nominative Singular.	अ आ इ ई उ ऊ ए ऐ ओ औ	आ ई ऊ ए ऐ ओ औ	ऊ ओ	अ इ ऊ	भ इ उ	अ भा इ उ	अ	अ			आ (या) ई (या) ऊ ऊ (वा)	ई (ये) ऊ (वे)	ऊ (वा)

☞ *Note* 1. This table might be profitably consulted along with the observations in Sec. 66.

2. The terminating vowels of the nominative singular, printed in small letters, denote that the words ending in them *do not usually* follow the declensions marked above them.

CHAPTER VI.

ADJECTIVE.

74. An adjective is a word which is joined to a noun, to describe or limit the thing expressed by it; as चांगला मुलगा a good boy; दोन घोडे two horses.

The adjectives which describe a noun are called *adjectives of quality* (गुणविशेषण), and those which limit it are called *adjectives of number*, or *numerals* (संख्याविशेषण or संख्यावाचक).

Adjectives of Quality.

75. Most adjectives are inflected to indicate their relation to the nouns which they qualify; thus,

(1) चांगला मुलगा a good boy, चांगली मुलगी a good girl, चांगलें घर a good house, indicating the gender.

(2) चांगले मुलगे good boys, चांगल्या मुलग्या good girls, चांगलीं घरें good houses, indicating the number.

(3) चांगल्या or } मुलग्याला or मुलगीला or घराला Sing.
    चांगले   } मुलग्यांला or मुलग्यांला or घरांला Plu., indicating the case.

76. Only the adjectives that end in आ are thus inflected in gender, number, and case before the noun: the rest do not modify their form; वाईट bad, पुरुष a man, m., or स्त्री, a woman, f., or लेंकरूं a child, n.; कडू bitter, भोंपळा a gourd, m., or भाजी vegetable, f., or औषध medicine, n.; गुणी मुलगा or मुलगी a virtuous boy or girl.

The form which the adjective assumes before an inflected noun is called the *attributive crude form*, विशेषण सामान्यरूप; as शहाण्या माणसाला to a wise man; वेड्या मुली जवळ by a mad girl. The attributive crude form ends in या or ए (or ये), as काळ्या or काळे माणसानें by a black man, and serves alike for all inflected nouns.

Note. Sometimes, in poetry, the adjective takes a case-form corresponding to that of the noun it qualifies; thus,

दास्य करावें भावें न असावें मानसें उदासीनें.

77. When adjectives of quality are used as independent words in the place of nouns, they are declined like nouns. They belong to the following declensions:—The adjectives ending in

(1) अ belong to the 2nd declension; वाईट bad, वाईटाला.
(2) आ belong to the 6th declension; तांबडा red, तांबड्याला.
(3) ई belong to the 1st declension; तांबडी, तांबडीला.
(4) उ belong to the 1st declension; कडू bitter, कडूला.
(5) ए belong to the 6th declension; वाकडें crooked, वाकड्याला.

Note. Sometimes, a distinct form in आ is derived from adjectives ending in अ, उ, &c., and then they become subject to the inflectional changes specified in Sec. 73; thus,

कडवा (कडू) bitter, m., कडवी f., कडवें n.

उंचा (उंच) high, m., उंची f., उंचें n.

लहाना (लहान) small, m., लहानी f., लहानें n.

The attributive crude forms of these adjectives terminate in अ, ए or या; लहान or लहाने or लहान्या मुलाला to a small boy.

78. The Marāṭhí adjectives have no degrees of comparison, or inflections to express their different degrees of signification.

Note. Sanskrit adjectives, introduced into the language, are sometimes inflected by means of affixes to express the comparative and superlative degrees respectively; thus, पुण्य moral, पुण्यतर more moral, पुण्यतम most moral. The terminations are, also, affixed to nouns; स्त्री a woman, स्त्रीतरा more of a woman. There are two more terminations, ईयस् and इष्ठ; as बलीयस् stronger, and बलिष्ठ strongest; तर and तरीन are Persian particles which Hindusthání words in the language, sometimes, assume; बेहतर better, बेहतरीन best, from बेह good. The English equivalents to these are "better" and "best."

Note. 1. In Marāṭhí the degrees of comparison are expressed by means of the particles हून, पेक्षां, परीस than; as रामाहून or रामापेक्षां or रामापरीस जगू श्याहाणा आहे Jagú is wiser than Rámá; जगू सर्वांहून श्याहाणा आहे Jagú is the wisest of all.

2. Also, by means of the adverb अधिक, more, placed before the adjective, to express the comparative degree, as अधिकचांगला better, and of the adverbs अति, परम, फार, extremely, placed before the adjective, to express the superlative degree, as परम चांगला, extremely good, best.

Examples of the Declension of Adjectives.

EXAMPLES.

चांगला m. Good (A good man).   चांगली f. Good (A good woman).

	Singular.	Plural.		Singular.	Plural.
Nom.	चांगला	चांगले	Nom.	चांगली	चांगल्या
Acc.	चांगला	चांगले	Acc.	चांगली	चांगल्या
Inst.	चांगल्यानें	चांगल्यानीं	Inst.	चांगलीनें	चांगल्यानीं
Dat.	चांगल्याला	चांगल्याला	Dat.	चांगलीला	चांगल्याला
Abl.	चांगल्याहून	चांगल्याहून	Abl.	चांगलीहून	चांगल्याहून
Gen.	चांगल्याचा	चांगल्याचा	Gen.	चांगलीचा	चांगल्याचा
Loc.	चांगल्यात	चांगल्यात	Loc.	चांगलींत	चांगल्यात
Attr.Cr.	चांगले or ल्या Sing. & Plu.		Attr.Cr.	चांगले or ल्या Sing. & Plu.	

चांगलें n. Good (A good thing).

	Singular.	Plural.
Nom.	चांगलें	चांगलीं
Acc.	चांगलें	चांगलीं
Inst.	चांगल्यानें	चांगल्यानीं &c., like the Masculine.

NUMERALS (संख्यावाचकें).

79. Most numerals are, in reality, adjectives, denoting *quantity*. Two classes of numerals only belong to adverbs. All numerals may be divided into *seven* classes.

(1) *Cardinal Numerals* (संख्यावाचकें), or those which simply denote the number of objects, and answer to the question *how many?* as एक one, दोन two, पन्नास fifty.

Note. In the compound cardinals, such as एकवीस twenty-one, &c., the smaller number comes first, while in English the smaller number comes last.

(2) *Ordinal numerals* (संख्यापूरकें), or those indicating the *order* or succession of objects; as पहिला first, दुसरा second, &c.

Note. The ordinals are formed from the cardinals (with the exception of पाहिला first, दुसरा second, तिसरा third, and चौथा fourth) by adding वा to the cardinals; as पांच five + वा = पांचवा fifth. But the ordinals from एकुणीस nineteen, and onwards, change the final vowel of the cardinal to आ before taking वा; एकुणिसावा nineteenth, शंभरावा hundredth.

(3) *Multiplicative numerals* (आवृत्तिवाचक), or those denoting *how many fold* a thing is; as एकपट one-fold or single, दुप्पट two-fold or double.

Note. The multiplicatives are formed from the numerals by adding पट fold to the cardinals, or एक + पट = एकपट one-fold; दोन two becomes दु before पट, and doubles the प, as दुप्पट; तीन becomes ति and प is doubled, as तिप्पट three-fold, चार becomes चौ, as चौपट four-fold; and दहा ten becomes दस, as दसपट ten-fold

(4) *Fractionals* (संख्यांशवाचकें), denoting *one or more parts* of a whole number; as सवा one-fourth.

(5) *Distributive numerals* (भेदवाचकें), or those which denote *how many each time*; as हरएक each, दरएक, प्रत्येक, &c.

(6) *Adverbial numerals of frequency* (संख्यावाचक क्रियाविशेषण अव्यय), or those denoting *how many times* a thing occurs; as एकदां once, दहादां ten times.

Note. They are formed by adding दां to the cardinal numerals.

(7) *Adverbial numerals of order* (क्रमवाचक क्रियाविशेषण अव्यय), denoting the order in which a thing occurs; पहिल्यानें or पहिल्यान, first or first time, दुसऱ्यानें or दुसऱ्यान second time, &c. They are the instrumental cases of the ordinal numeral adjectives.

80. The following is a table of the Numerals:—

Cardinal Numbers.

1	१	एक, येक.	6	६	सहा.
2	२	दोन.	7	७	सात.
3	३	तीन.	8	८	आठ.
4	४	चार.	9	९	नऊ, नव.
5	५	पांच.	10	१०	दहा.

11	११	अकरा.	43	४३	त्रेचाळीस.
12	१२	बारा.	44	४४	चव्वेचाळीस.
13	१३	तेरा.	45	४५	पंचेचाळीस.
14	१४	चवदा, चौदा.	46	४६	शोचाळीस.
15	१५	पंधरा.	47	४७	सत्तेचाळीस.
16	१६	सोळा.	48	४८	अठ्ठेचाळीस.
17	१७	सत्रा.	49	४९	एकुणपन्नास.
18	१८	अठरा.	50	५०	पन्नास.
19	१९	एकुणीस.	51	५१	एकावन्न.
20	२०	वीस.	52	५२	बावन्न.
21	२१	एकवीस.	53	५३	त्रेपन्न.
22	२२	बावीस, बेवीस.	54	५४	चौपन्न, चोपन.
23	२३	तेवीस.	55	५५	पंचावन्न.
24	२४	चोवीस, चौवीस, च-	56	५६	छपन्न.
25	२५	पंचवीस. [व्वीस.	57	५७	सत्तावन्न.
26	२६	सव्वीस.	58	५८	अठ्ठावन्न.
27	२७	सत्तावीस.	59	५९	एकुणसाठ.
28	२८	अठ्ठावीस.	60	६०	साठ.
29	२९	एकुणतीस.	61	६१	एकसष्ट.
30	३०	तीस.	62	६२	बासष्ट.
31	३१	एकतीस.	63	६३	त्रेसष्ट.
32	३२	बत्तीस	64	६४	चवसष्ट, चौसष्ट.
33	३३	तेतीस, तेहतीस.	65	६५	पांसष्ट.
34	३४	चवतीस, चौतीस.	66	६६	सासष्ट.
35	३५	पस्तीस.	67	६७	सदसष्ट, सत्सष्ट.
36	३६	छत्तीस.	68	६८	अठुसष्ट, अडुसष्ट.
37	३७	सत्तीस, सनतीस.	69	६९	एकुणहत्तर.
38	३८	अडतीस अठतीस.	70	७०	सत्तर.
39	३९	एकुणचाळीस.	71	७१	एकाहत्तर, एकेहत्तर.
40	४०	चाळीस.	72	७२	बाहत्तर.
41	४१	एकेचाळीस.	73	७३	त्रेहत्तर, त्र्याहत्तर.
42	४२	बेचाळीस.	74	७४	चौऱ्याहत्तर.

(44)

75	७५	पंचेहत्तर.	88	८८	अइचाय्शी.
76	७६	शाहत्तर, शेहत्तर.	89	८९	एकुणनब्बद, नव्यायशी.
77	७७	सत्याहत्तर, सत्तेहत्तर.	90	९०	नव्बद.
78	७८	अव्याहत्तर, अड़ेहत्तर.	91	९१	एक्याणव.
79	७९	एकुणॅऍशी.	92	९२	ब्याणव.
80	८०	ऍशी.	93	९३	ड्याणव.
81	८१	एक्यायशी.	94	९४	चौन्याण्णव.
82	८२	ब्यायशी.	95	९५	चाण्णव.
83	८३	ड्यायशी.	96	९६	शाण्णव.
84	८४	चौन्यायशी.	97	९७	सत्याण्णव.
85	८५	पंचायशी.	98	९८	अठ्याण्णव.
86	८६	शायशी.	99	९९	नव्याण्णव.
87	८७	सत्यायशी.	100	१००	शंभर.

101	१०१	एकोत्तरशें, एकशेंएक.
102	१०२	दुवोत्तरशें, एकशें दोन.
200	२००	दोनशें.
300	३००	तीनशें.
400	४००	चारशें.
500	५००	पाचशें.
1000	१०००	हजार, सहस्र.
10000	१००००	दहाहजार, दशसहस्र.
100000	१०००००	लाख, लक्ष.
1000000	१००००००	दहालाख, दशलक्ष.
10000000	१०००००००	कोटि, क्रोड.

Ordinal Numbers.

1st	१	पहिला.	5th	५	पांचवा.
2nd	२	दुसरा.	6th	६	सहावा.
3rd	३	तिसरा.	7th	७	सातवा.
4th	४	चवथा.	8th	८	आठवा.

FRACTIONAL NUMBERS.

$\frac{1}{4}$	·|·	पाव.
$\frac{1}{2}$	·||·	अर्धा-र्धी-र्धें, &c.
$\frac{3}{4}$	·|||·	पाऊण.
$1\frac{1}{4}$	१|·	सव्वा.
$1\frac{1}{2}$	१||·	दीड.
$1\frac{3}{4}$	१|||·	पावणेदोन, पाउणेदोन.
$2\frac{1}{4}$	२|·	सव्वादोन.
$2\frac{1}{2}$	२||·	अडीच.
$2\frac{3}{4}$	२|||·	पावणेतीन, पाउणेतीन.
$3\frac{1}{4}$	३|·	सव्वातीन.
$3\frac{1}{2}$	३||·	साडेतीन.
$3\frac{3}{4}$	३|||·	पावणेचार, पाउणेचार.

शेंकडों By hundreds. हज़ारों By thousands. लाखों By myriads.

Examples of the Declension of Numerals.

एक One.

	Singular Masculine.	Singular Feminine.
Nom.	एक	एक
Acc.	एक	एक
Inst.	एकानें	एकीनें
Dat.	एकाला	एकीला
Abl.	एकाहून	एकीहून
Gen.	एकाचा	एकीचा
Loc.	एकांत	एकींत
Attr. Cr.	एक, एका, एके, एक्या.	

The numerals दोन two, तीन three, and चार four, are changed to दोहों, तिहों, चोहों or चौहों, in order to make up their crude forms, and these crude forms answer for the three genders. Thus,—

Plural.

	m. f. n.		m. f. n.
Nom. & Acc.	दोन Two. तीन Three	Nom. & Acc.	चार Four.
Inst.	दोंहींनीं. तिहींनीं.	Inst.	चोंहींनीं.
Dat.	दोंहोंला-ना. तिहींला-ना.	Dat.	चोंहोंला-ना.
Attr. Cr.	दोंहों or दोन. तिहों or तीन.	Attr. Cr.	चोंहों or चार.

When दोन, तीन, चार refer to a noun denoting a *person*, they assume these forms for the three genders:—

Plural.	दोघे m.	दोघी f.	दोघें n.
"	तिघे m.	तिघी f.	तिघें n.
"	चोघे m.	चोघी f.	चोघें n.

The masculine and neuter forms are declined like the nouns of the fifth declension, and the feminine like the nouns of the first. Thus,

Plural.

Nom. and Acc.	दोघे m.	दोघी f.
Inst.	दोघांनीं.	दोघींनीं.
Dat.	दोघांला or ना.	दोघींला or ना.
Attr. Cr.	दोघां or दोघों.	दोघीं or दोघों.

In the same way are the other numerals तिघे, चोघे, declined.

The ordinals पहिला first, m., पहिली f., पहिलें n.; दुसरा second, m., दुसरी f., दुसरें n.; विसावा twentieth, m., विसावी f., विसावें n., &c.; and all other numerals ending in आ m., ई f., and एं n., are declined like चांगला m., good, चांगली, चांगलें (Sec. 68).

CHAPTER VII.
PRONOUNS.

81. A Pronoun is a word which supplies the place of a noun, or refers to a noun mentioned either before or after it; as मी I, जो मनुष्य The man who.

There are six kinds of pronouns:—Personal, Reflexive, Relative, Interrogative, Demonstrative, and Indefinite.

82. The personal pronouns are the principal pronouns, being substitutes for proper names. They represent three persons, viz., the *speaker*, the *person spoken to*, and the *person spoken of*. The other pronouns, being subordinate to these, are also supposed to have three persons, although their forms do not vary.

83. All pronouns, like nouns, have three genders and two numbers; of these a few have no distinct forms to distinguish the gender and the number.

84. ☞ Like adjectives, *it is only those pronouns that end* in आ m. or ओ m. that have three gender forms; the rest have not.

Note. आ is the modern modification of the Prákṛit ओ m. which is, in its turn, a modification of the Sanskṛit Visarga (:). ओ is the terminating vowel of words in old Maráthí books, and is still used in Gujaráti. Thus,

Sans. घोट:, Prák. घोडो, Mar. घोडा, Guj. घोडो A horse.

85. The pronouns are generally declined only in six cases, *i. e.*, not in the accusative and the vocative.

The case-terminations and the postpositions are affixed either to the dative crude form, or to the genitive-case crude form. It is the instrumental and ablative cases alone that inflect the genitive case; as त्याच्यानें By him, माझ्याहून Than I.

When pronouns stand before inflected nouns, they terminate in या, like adjectives (Sec. 69); as त्या भटानें By that Bhaṭ (priest). The form which they assume before an inflected noun would be called the *attributive crude form of a pronoun.*

Note. The first and second personal pronouns are very irregularly declined.

I. Personal Pronouns.

86. The personal pronouns are substitutes for the names of persons. They are three in number; as मी I, तूं Thou, तो He (ती She

तें It); and represent three persons, the first, second, and third. They have distinct plural forms, but the first and second personal forms do not distinguish the sex. Thus,

1st Pers. Sing.	मी m. f. n.		Plu.	आम्ही m. f. n.
2nd ,,	तूं or तु m. f. n.		,,	तुम्ही m. f. n.
3rd ,,	तो m. ती f. तें n.		,,	ते m. त्या f. तीं n.

Note. The third personal forms are identical with the forms of the Demonstrative pronoun तो That.

मी I.

Nom. Singular	मी I.
Inst. ,,	मीं or म्यां By me.
,,	मसीं or मजसीं Against me.
Dat. ,,	मला or मज or मजला To me.
Abl. ,,	मजहून Than me.
Gen. ,,	माझा m. माझी, माझें Of me, *or* my, *or* mine.
Loc. ,,	माझ्यांत In me.
Attr. Cr. ,,	मज

आम्ही We.

Nom. Plural	आम्हो We.
Inst. ,,	आम्हीं By us.
	आम्हासीं Against us.
Dat. ,,	आम्हाला or आम्हास To us.
Abl. ,,	आम्हाहून Than us.
Gen. ,,	आमचा, आमची, आमचें, Of us.
Loc. ,,	आम्हांत In us.
Attr. Cr. ,,	आम्हा.

तूं Thou.

	Singular.			Plural.	
Nom.	तूं	Thou.	Nom.	तुह्मी	You.
Inst.	तूं or त्वां	By thee.	Inst.	तुह्मीं	By you.
	तुसीं or तुजसीं	Against thee.	,,	तुह्मासीं	Against you.
Dat.	तुला or तुजला	To thee.	Dat.	तुह्माला or तुह्मास	To you.
Abl.	तुजहून	From thee.	Abl.	तुह्माहून	From you.
Gen.	तुझा, तुझी, तुझें	Of thee, *or* thy, *or* [thine.	Gen.	तुमचा-ची-चें	Of you.
Loc.	तुइयांत	In thee.	Loc.	तुह्मांत	In you.
Attr. Cr.	तुज		Attr. Cr.	तुह्मा.	

Note. The crude forms मज and तुज are not used before a noun in the instrumental case; the instrumental case forms of the pronouns are used; as म्यां रामानें By me, Rámá; त्वां मुलीनें By thee, a girl. मज ब्राह्मणाला दान द्यावें Alms should be given to me, a Bráhmaṇ. आह्मां गरीब लोकांची अद्द्दी समजून झालो We poor people understood so. In the plural, however, the attributive crude form is used before the instrumental case; तुह्मा लोकांनीं By you people.

II. Reflexive Pronoun.

87. The Reflexive Pronouns are substituted for substantives chiefly when the substantives are subjects of reflexive verbs; रामानें आपणास (रामाला) मारून घेतलें Rámá killed himself.

There are two reflexive pronouns, आपण and स्वतः one's self.

Note. आपण is always a pronoun, but स्वतः is often an adverb; स्वतः तुह्माला गेलें पाहिजे you must go personally. The genitive of आपण is used as an expletive particle, called in Hindusthání *takyá kalám,* or pillow-word; as मी आपला येथून उठलों तों आपला त्याच्या घरीं गेलों.

88. The reflexive pronouns are employed in reference to nouns or pronouns of all persons, genders, and numbers. आपण is often used by a person when he speaks of himself and of others with respect. It is then equivalent to the English "we," "your honour," "his honour," &c.; as आपण जर इतकें माझें कार्य कराल If you will do this thing for me, &c.; मग आपण निघून गेले Then he went away. आपण is, in fact, the

only form which gentlemen should use in speaking *to* and *of* a gentleman.

89. आपण is thus declined :—

आपण Self or Oneself.

Nom. Sing. & Plur.	आपण Self.
Inst.	,,	आपण By self.
	,,	आपणाशीं Against self.
Dat.	,,	आपणाला or आपणास To self.
Abl.	,,	आपणाहून From self.
Gen.	,,	आपला, आपली, आपलें Of self.
Loc.	,,	आपणांत In self.
Attr. Cr.	,,	आपणा.

Note. आपला is often used for आपण, as आपल्यास or आपल्याला for आपणास or आपणाला, which is a gross error. आपल्याला would mean To my own (son, &c.)

III. Relative Pronoun.

90. The Relative Pronoun refers or relates to another word or phrase in a sentence; as जो मुलगा येणार होता The boy who was to come.

There is only one relative pronoun, viz., जो Who, having its feminine and neuter forms जी and जें respectively.

91. There are other relative pronouns, derived from जो, which are thus classified :—

(1) *Relatives of quantity* : जितका, जितकाला ; जेवढा जेवढाला As much, or As many.

Note. जितका = जो + इतका ; जेवढा = जो + एवढा.

(2) *Relatives of kind* : जसा, जसला, जसलाला, As (implying sort or kind).

Note. जसा = जो + असा.

(3) *Relatives of order*: जिनकाया, जेवढावा As much (in a series).

92. The relative forms जो who, m., जी who, f., and जें which, n., are thus declined :—

	Masculine.	Feminine.	Neuter.
Nom. Sing.	जो who.	जी who.	जें which.
Inst. ,,	ज्यानें, ज्यानें, जेंनें	जिनें, जिनें	The oblique
Dat. ,,	ज्यास, ज्याला	जिला, जीस, जिजस	forms are like
Abl. ,,	ज्याहून	जिहून, जिजहून	the masculine.
Gen. ,,	ज्याचा-ची-चें	जिचा-ची-चें	
Loc. ,,	ज्यान	जींन	
Attr. Cr. ,,	ज्या	ज्या	

	Masculine.	Feminine.	Neuter.
Nom. Plu.	जे	ज्या	जीं
Inst. ,,	ज्यानीं		
Dat. ,,	ज्यास, ज्याला, ज्याना		
Abl. ,,	ज्याहून		
Gen. ,,	ज्यांचा-ची-चें		
Loc. ,,	ज्यात		
Attr. Cr. ,,	ज्या		

Note. ज्या is written also जा; as जाला To whom.

IV. Demonstrative Pronoun.

93. The Demonstrative Pronoun distinctly designates the word to which it refers; as तो माणूस That man.

The demonstrative pronouns are हा This, pointing to an object near to the speaker, and तो That, pointing to a distant object.

Both these pronouns have separate gender and number forms; हा This, m., ही f., हें n., Sing.; हे m., ह्या f., हीं n., Plu.; तो That, m., ती f., तें n. Sing.; ते m., त्या f., तीं n., Plu.

94. There are several forms derived from these pronouns, which are these:—

(1) *Demonstrative of quantity:* इतका, इतकाला, एवढा, एवढाला, This much; तितका, तितकाला, तेवढा, तेवढाला That much.

(2) *Demonstrative of sort:* असा, असला, असलाला This like; तसा, तसला, तसलाला That like.

(3) *Demonstrative of order:* इतकावा, एवढावा This much (in a series); तितकावा, तेवढावा That much.

95. The demonstratives हा This, and तो That, are thus declined:—

Singular.

	Mas.	Fem.	Neut.
Nom.	हा	ही	हें
Inst.	ह्यानें, ह्यानें	हिनें, हिणें	The same as the masculine.
Dat.	ह्यास, ह्याला, ह्याजला	हिला, हीस, हिजला	
Abl.	ह्याहून	हिहून	
Gen.	ह्याचा-ची-चें	हिचा-ची-चें	
Loc.	ह्यांत	हींत	
Attr. Cr.	ह्या	ह्या.	

Plural.

	Mas.	Fem.	Neut.
Nom.	हे	ह्या	हीं
Inst.		ह्यांनीं-णीं	
Dat.		ह्यांस-ला-ना	
Abl.		ह्याहून	
Gen.		ह्यांचा-ची-चें	
Loc.		ह्यांत	
Attr. Cr.		ह्या	

Singular.

	Mas.	Fem.	Neut.
Nom.	तो	ती	तें
Inst.	त्यानें, त्यानें	तिनें, तिनें	The same as the
Dat.	त्याला, त्यास	तिला, तीस	masculine.
Abl.	त्याहून	तिहून	
Gen.	त्याचा-ची-चें	तिचा-ची-चें	
Loc.	त्यांत	तींत	
Attr. Cr.	त्या	ता	

Plural.

	Mas.	Fem.	Neut.
Nom.	ते	त्या	तीं

Inst.	त्यानीं, त्याणीं
Dat.	त्यांस, त्याला, त्यांना
Abl.	त्याहून
Gen.	त्यांचा-ची-चें
Loc.	त्यांत
Attr. Cr.	त्यां

The forms असा, असला, इतका, एवढा, तेवढा, तेवढाला, &c., and their neuters, follow the sixth declension, and the feminines, the first.

Note. In the demonstrative oblique forms, या and इ are employed in the place of ह्या and हि; त्यानें or यानें, हिनें or इनें. Of these two forms the latter is considered preferable.

V. Interrogative Pronoun.

96. Interrogative pronouns are used to form questions; as कोण आहे? Who is there?

They are used as substantives; as कोण बोलतो? Who is speaking?— or as adjectives; as कोण माणूस? What man?

The interrogative pronouns are these: कोण Who? कोणता Which one? काय What? किती How many?

There are several other forms, which are as follows:—

(1) *Interrogatives of sort*: कसा, कसला, कसचा, कसकसा Which like?
Note. कः S. + असा = कसा.

(2) *Interrogatives of order*: कितवा, How much (in a series)?

(3) *Interrogatives of magnitude*: किनका, किनकाला, केवढा, केवढाला How much?

97. The interrogatives are thus declined :—

कोण Who, m. f.

		Sing.		Plu.	
Nom.		कोण		कोण	
Inst.	,,	कोणीं, कोणें	,,	कोणीं	
Dat.	,,	कोणा, कोणाला	,,	कोणा, कोणाला	
Abl.	,,	कोणाहून	,,	कोणाहून	
Gen.	,,	कोणाचा-ची-चें	,,	कोणाचा-ची-चें	
Loc.	,,	कोणांत	,,	कोणांत	
Attr. Cr.		कोणा, कोणे, कोण्या Sing. and Plu.			

Note. कोण्या is preferable before feminine nouns, and कोणा before particles; as कोणाजवळ Near whom?

काय What?

		Sing.		Plu.	
Nom.		काय		काय	
Inst.	,,	कशानें	,,	कशानीं, &c.	

Note. कइया is preferable before a feminine noun.

VI. Indefinite Pronoun.

98. The Indefinite Pronouns express an indefinite generality.

They are कोण, कोणी Some one; अमुक, अमका, फलाणा A certain one; उभय Both; काहीं, Something; अन्य, इतर, वरकड Other; अवघा, सर्व All.

Of these pronouns, those ending in अ follow the second declension, those in आ, the sixth, and those in ई, the first.

CHAPTER VIII.
THE ADVERB.

99. An Adverb is a word used to modify the sense of a verb, participle, adjective, or another adverb, and is usually placed near it; तो चांगलें लिहितो He writes well; ती फार शहाणी आहे She is very wise.

100. Adverbs are either declined or undeclined. Those adverbs alone are declined which end in एं; thus, तो बरें बोलतो He speaks well.

Note. Adjectives and pronouns are often employed to modify verbs, and those of them which end in आ m. have the neuter form in एं: this neuter form is identical with the adverbial form in एं; बरा good, बरी f., बरें n.

The Declinable Adverbs agree in gender and number with the uninflected subject or object of the verb which they modify; as तो चांगला गाईल He will sing well; ती गायन चांगलें करिती She sings well. But it retains its own form in the following instances :—

(1) When the subject of the intransitive verb is omitted; होईल कसें? How will it be?

(2) When the subject of the intransitive verb is inflected; त्यानें जावें तरी कसें? How could he go?

(3) When both the subject and the object of the transitive verb are inflected; त्यानें त्याला कसें मारावें? How could he beat him?

Note. The adverbs of quality are compared like adjectives; ती मजपेक्षां चांगली गा ये She sings better than I. (See Sec. 78.)

(56)

The Undeclinable Adverbs, called Particles, are enumerated in Chapter XIII.

101. The inflected forms of the adverb in एं are the following:—

Sing. चांगला m., चांगली f., चांगलें n.
Plu. चांगले m., चांगल्या f., चांगलीं n.

CHAPTER IX.
THE VERB.

A Verb is the chief word in a sentence, and expresses either the being or the action of any thing.

I. The Classification of Verbs.

102. Verbs are classified, *first*, according to their *signification*, and, *secondly*, according to their *form* and *conjugation*.

I. Verbs are divided according to their signification, into *two* classes, viz., *the Transitive* and *Intransitive*.

(1) A verb is called *Transitive* (सकर्मक) when the action denoted by it passes on to the object; मुलगा पोथी वाचितो The boy reads a book.

(2) A verb is called *Intransitive* (अकर्मक) when the action terminates in the subject; मी चालतों I walk.

Note. Several verbs are both transitive and intransitive (उभयविध); as त्यानें झाड मोडिलें He broke the tree; झाड मोडलें The tree broke.

II. Verbs are divided into the following *seven* classes, according to their *form* and *conjugation* :—

(1) *Simple verbs* (सिद्ध), or verbs that are not derived from any other verb in the language; तो काम करितो He does work.

(2) *Causal verbs* (प्रयोज्य), or verbs which are derived from simple verbs by the aid of the suffix वि, to indicate that the action denoted by

them is performed by the agent through the instrumentality of another individual; as तो काम करविनो He causes the work to be done (by another).

(3) *Potential verbs* (शक्य), or verbs which are derived from a simple verb by the addition of व, to denote that the agent has power or ability to do the action indicated by them; त्याच्यानें काम करवतें He can do the work.

(4) *Irregular verbs* (अनियमित), or verbs which are irregularly conjugated in the past tense; as मी करितों I do, म्यां केलें I did.

(5) *Anomalous verbs* (विधिभंजक), or verbs which are irregularly conjugated in all the tenses and constructions; मी शिकतों I learn, मी ग्रंथ शिकलों I learnt the book.

Note. There are other verbs which might be called semi-anomalous, since they are irregularly conjugated in all the tenses, but regularly in the constructions; as मी सांगेन I shall tell. There are others, again, which are regularly conjugated in the tenses, but irregularly in the constructions; ती भात जेवली She ate the rice. They might be called *anti-semi-anomalous* verbs. Of both these classes there are less than a dozen words in the language.

(6) *Defective verbs* (गौण), or verbs which are wanting in some forms of conjugation; पाहिजे I want.

(7) *Compound verbs* (संयुक्त), or verbs made up of two or more words; जेवूं पालणें To feed.

II. The Inflection of Verbs.

103. In the inflection of verbs are distinguished—

(1) *Two Numbers*: singular and plural.

(2) *Three Genders*: masculine, feminine, and neuter.

(3) *Three Persons*: first person, second person, and third person.

(4) *Three Leading Tenses*: present, past, and future.

(5) *Five Moods*: indicative, subjunctive, imperative, conditional, and infinitive.

(6) *Two Verbal Substantives, four Verbal Adjectives,* and *four Participles.*

(7) *Three Prayogas* or Constructions: *Kartari* or subjective, *Karmaṇi* or objective, and *Bhávi* or neuter.

(8) *Two Voices*: active and passive.

The Tenses.

104. Tenses are forms of verbs indicating the *time* of the action or event signified by them; as मी मोडितों I break; म्यां मोडिलें I broke.

105. A Maráthí verb is capable of expressing four times by means of mere inflections, and the forms it assumes are called *Simple Tenses*; as मी चालतों I walk; मी चाललों I walked; मी चालें I was wont to walk; मी चालेन I shall walk.

When tenses are formed by the aid of other verbs, called Auxiliary verbs, or helping verbs, they are called *Compound Tenses*; as मी चालत आहें I am walking. We shall consider these separately. (Chapter XII.)

106. The simple tenses are the present, the past, the past habitual, and the future.

(1) The present tense (वर्तमानकाळ) expresses action or being in the present time; as मी लिहितों I write.

Note a. It indicates an act which has lately commenced, and is in a state of progression; नू थट्टा करितोस You are jesting.

b. It indicates an action that is just about to commence; चल मी तुला कांहीं मौज दाखवितों Come, I will show you something strange.

c. An action that will certainly happen in some future time; उद्यां सकाळपासून तुझ्यास मोकळीक देतों I will give you free leave tomorrow, the whole day, from morning to evening.

d. A general truth; जो आपल्या मुखानें आपलो स्तुति करितो तो लघुत्व पायतो He who with his own mouth spreads abroad his own fame is sure to meet with contempt.

e. An act long since past, but present at the time referred to in the discourse; भोजराजा विचारितो Bhoj Rájá asks. This is called the historical present tense.

(2) The past tense (भूतकाळ) expresses an action as completed in time already past or spent; as मी बोललों I spoke.

Note. This is the Greek aorist, which expresses an action as completed in past time, but leaves it in other respects wholly indefinite.

Note. This form expresses conditionality with जर If, expressed or understood; कधीं तूं आमच्या दारावरून आलास तर मजकडे ये Shouldst thou ever pass our door, come to me.

(3) The habitual past tense (रीतिभूतकाळ) indicates the habitual doing of an action in past time; as तो बाहेर निघे व कमरेस चार पांच चिरगुटें बांधी He was in the habit of sallying forth, and tying four or five pieces of cloth around his loins.

Note. It is used sometimes in the subordinate clause of a complex sentence, when it signifies that the completion of one act was the measure of the continuance of the other; as तीं मुलें भो येई तोंवर जेवलीं Those children ate till they had arrived at the very point of vomiting.

Note. In old Maráthí this form was employed for the present, past, and future indicative; as तो करी = तो करितो He does, or तो करिता झाला He did, or तो करील He will do.

(4) The future tense (भविष्यकाळ) expresses an action to occur in time subsequent to the present; as मी मरून देवाजवळ जाईन After I die I shall go to God.

Note. Besides this general sense, the future has various other senses, a few of which are the following:—

a. It expresses an act which at a particular past time was considered about to happen; as आम्ही प्रतिक्षणीं भिऊं कीं तूं आतां मरसील. We were every moment afraid that you would instantly die.

b. It expresses the incumbency of a particular act; as कां पळेन? Why should I run?

c. It expresses potentiality; as त्यास दात आले नाहींत, तो खाईल कसा? He has got no teeth yet, how then can he eat?

d. It expresses, also, past potentiality; मुलखांत पांडव कोठून असतील? How could the Pándavás (the sons of Pandu) spread abroad over the whole country?

Moods.

107. Moods are forms of verbs expressing the manner of the being or action signified by them; तो करिता If he did; तो येतो He comes.

108. There are five moods in Maráthí, viz., the Indicative (स्वार्थ), the Subjunctive (विध्यर्थ), the Imperative (आज्ञार्थ), the Conditional (संकेतार्थ), and the Infinitive (सामान्यार्थ).

(1) The indicative indicates, that is, affirms or denies; तूं चालतोस You walk. It is also used in asking questions; तो येईल काय? Will he come?

(2) The subjunctive mood expresses duty or obligation, and is known in English by the signs "should" or ought," as well as "may or "might;" ड्याचा अपराध केला असेल त्यापासीं क्षमा मागावी You ought to beg pardon of the person you have offended.

Note. Besides this general sense of fitness or propriety, the subjunctive mood has the following significations:—

a. Ground or reason; राजा नेमावा म्हणून सर्व पक्षी एकत्र झाले होते All the fowls had assembled that they might elect a king.

b. Habitual act; त्यापासून कोणास उपद्रव नसे, त्याला फारच कंटाळा आणिला तर मात्र त्यानें पिसाळावें In general he hurt nobody; only when he was excessively teased he would become outrageous.

c. Inquiry; आतां आपण काय करावें? What shall we do now?

d. Wish; ईश्वरानें तुझ्यास शतगुणित फल द्यावें May God repay you a hundred-fold!

e. Command; आतां तुम्हीं जावें You may go now.

(3) The imperative mood expresses command, advice, exhortation, or benediction: तूं आपलें काम कर Do your own business; चला माडीवर जाऊं Come, let us go upstairs; या सख्यांनो Come away, my friends; ईश्वर तुमचें कल्याण करो! May God bless you!

(4) The conditional mood expresses a condition or supposition; as असें जर तुला झणतां तर त्यावेळीं तुझ्यानें त्याची थट्टा करवती? If he had spoken

to you in that manner, could you then have mocked him? हा हिंवाळा न येता आणि पावसाळाच राहता तर बरें होतें Were that winter never to come, and the rainy season always to remain, it would be delightful.

Note. The conditional is chiefly used if things are spoken of that might have possibly happened, but which have not actually taken place. To denote an actual possibility the indicative is generally used; as त्याला औषध द्याल तर तुमचा उपकार जन्मभर विसरणार नाहीं If you would have the goodness to give him medicine I shall never forget your kindness as long as I live.

(5) The infinitive mood expresses the action of the verb without any limitation of number, person, &c.; आम्हास उपासीं मरूं देऊं नका Do not allow us to die of hunger. The supine in आयास is generally used in its place; तो उपासानें मरूं or मरायास लागला He began to die of starvation.

Verbal Nouns and Participles.

(धातुसाधितें).

109. These are the *Gerund* and *Supine*, the *Participial Adjectives*, and the *Participles*.

They are derived from verbs, and relate action to nouns without directly affirming it of them.

Note. There are several other words derived from verbs, which are not included here, since they do not convey the notion of action; they are enumerated in one of the chapters on Derivation.

110. The Gerund is a verbal neuter substantive, expressing state or action in a general way; as करणें To do, or doing; वाचणें झाल्यानंतर तो म्हणाला After the reading was over, he said.

Note. Like the English gerund, it takes an accusative object; तूं मला पन्नास सुपाऱ्या देणें आहेस You have to give me (or you owe me) fifty betelnuts; मग जें करणें असेल तें कर Then do what you intend doing.

Note. In the latter example the gerund is nominative to असेल, and takes the accusative object जें.

Note: It, sometimes, expresses a command; पत्र लिहीत जाणें Continue to write to us.

Note. It is used as a noun to give name to the verb; as करणें धातु The verb to do.

It is declined like a noun of the sixth declension in all the cases. Thus,—

करणें To do.

Sing.	Nom.	करणें	Doing.	Plu.	Nom.	करणीं
,,	Instr.	करण्यानें	By doing.	,,	Inst.	करण्यानीं
,,	Dat.	करण्यास-ला	To doing.	,,	Dat.	करण्यास-ना
,,	Abl.	करण्याहून	From doing.	,,	Abl.	करण्याहून
,,	Gen.	करण्याचा-ची-चें	Of doing.	,,	Gen.	करण्याचा
,,	Loc.	करण्यांत	In doing.	,,	Loc.	करण्यांत

111. The Supine is another verbal neuter noun, signifying action in a particular state, as in Maráthí, in the particular state of propriety or duty; as आह्मांस देशांतरीं जावें लागेल We shall be under the necessity of going abroad.

It is declined only in the dative and the genitive singular, and has two distinct forms for each case. Thus,

जावें It is necessary to go.

Nom. Sing. जावें

Dat. ,, जावयास-ला or जायास-ला

Gen. ,, जावयाचा-ची-चें or जायाचा-ची-चें

☞ *Note*. जावें is a verb in the subjunctive mood when it is joined to a noun or pronoun in the instrumental case, but when it is related to a noun or pronoun denoting agency in the dative case, it is a supine; as त्यानें जावें or जावें होतें He should have gone; त्याला जावें लागेल He should have to go. The latter is the supine.

Note. The supine is generally used in the oblique forms. In the dative it has much the same meaning as the infinitive, and most verbs take it rather than the infinitive; तें मी करावयास सिद्ध आहें I am ready to do that. In the genitive it is often interchangeable with the gerund; as आह्मांस देशांतरीं जायाचें or जाण्याचें

पडेल We shall be under the necessity of going abroad; करावयाची or करण्याची प्रेरणा incitement to action.

Note. The supine is used, also, to make up the compound forms of the moods and tenses.

112. The Participial Adjectives are participles used as adjectives; as जळत Burning, जळतें घर The burning house. They are the following :—

(1) The present participial adjective, ending in ता m.; जळता वांसा A burning post.

(2) The past participial adjective, ending in लेला m.; as मेलेलें जनावर A dead animal.

(3) The future participial adjective, ending in णारा m.; as येणारे लोक The people intending to come.

(4) The participial adjective of currency, ending in ऊ; as चालू कायदा The current law, the law in force at the present time.

Note. Those participial adjectives that end in आ m. are declined like the ordinary adjectives in आ m.

Note. The participial adjectives are modifications of the participles given below.

113. The Participles are the present, the past, the past conjunctive or pluperfect, and the future. They are chiefly used to make up compound tenses.

(1) The present participle denotes currency of action, and has three forms, viz., त, ता, and ताना.

Note. a. The form in त when compounded with other verbs, expresses the principal idea in the mind of the speaker; देवास भजत जा Go on worshipping God; तूं स्वतां उद्योग करीत ऐस Do yourself continue to work diligently.

b. The form in ता is used to make up a subordinate clause, and expresses an act less important than that signified by the verb of the principal clause; as त्यांला न कळतां मागून जाऊन उभा राहिला Without their knowledge, he went after them and stood concealed.

c. The form in तानां is of the same import as that in ता, but a little more emphatic; as बारा बाजतां or बाजतानां ये Come at twelve o'clock; आज दहा दिवस तिला फिरतानां पहातों I have seen her these ten days going about.

(2) The past participle denotes past time, and is used to make up compound tenses. It ends in ला or लेला. The former is chiefly used to make up compound tenses, and the latter as a participial adjective.

(3) The past conjunctive ends in ऊन, and occasionally in ओन, and denotes an action that takes place before that mentioned in the principal clause; as मामा पुढें जाऊन पायां पडेन I will go into the presence of my uncle, and on my knees beg his pardon; गाणें होऊन कांहीं दिवस राहील After the singing is over, still a part of the day will remain.

Note. The participle in ऊन has, sometimes, an adverbial force; as तें मी जाणून आहें That I know full well.

Note. Sometimes it has the force of a conditional participle; पहा मी जाणना असून इतका घाबरलों See what a blunder I have committed, wise man as I am!

Note. It is frequently used with the verbs टाकणें Throw away, दे Give, &c., to make an imperative form; as फेंकून दे Fling it away, धुऊन टाक Wash it thoroughly. The imperative verb gives only a sort of completeness to the action.

(4) The future participle ends in णार, and is used to make compound tenses; तो येणार आहे He is to come, implying that the speaker has some knowledge of an intention to come.

Note. This participle is used for the verbal noun of agency; येणाराला, and not येणाऱ्याला, To the taker.

Constructions (प्रयोग).

114. We must anticipate Syntax to a certain extent to understand the *Prayogas*, a knowledge of which is essential to conjugation.

The verb in Maráthí agrees in gender, number, and person, either with its subject or object, or with neither: this agreement or disagreement of the verb with the subject or the object is indicated by the form of the sentence: this form or mode of construction is called *Prayoga* by the Maráthí grammarians.

115. There are three modes of construction, or *Prayogas*, viz., the *Kartari* (कर्तरि), *Karmaṇi* (कर्मणि), and the *Bhávi* (भावी).

(1) The *Kartari Prayoga* denotes that the verb agrees with the subject (कर्ता); as रामा चालतो Rámá walks; ती रडतो She cries. This is the *subjective construction*.

(2) The *Karmaṇi Prayoga* denotes that the verb agrees with the object (कर्म); त्यानें पोथी वाचिली He read the book: मुलीनें भात खाल्ला The girl has eaten the rice. This is the *objective construction*.

(3) The *Bhávi Prayoga* denotes that the verb agrees neither with the subject nor the object, but is conjugated in the neuter singular; त्यानें त्याला मारिलें He beat him. This is the neuter (neither of the two) construction.

Note. In the Bhávi construction, the verb may be either transitive or intransitive. When it is transitive, the construction is called सकर्मक भावी, and when it is intransitive, the construction is called अकर्मक भावी; (1) त्यानें जावें He may go; (2) त्यानें त्याला मारिलें He beat him.

In the subjective construction, the subject is in the nominative case, *i. e.*, it is uninflected; in the objective construction, the subject is in an oblique case; and in the neuter construction, both the subject and the object are in an oblique case.

The inflected subject is either in the instrumental or the dative case; त्यानें खाल्लें He ate; त्याला खाववतें He can eat. It is also in the genitive instrumental; as त्याच्यानें जाववतें He can go. The inflected object is in the dative case only; as त्यानें त्याला दिलें He gave it to him.

Note. All verbs, excepting the potentials, generally take the subjective construction in the present and future tenses.

The intransitives and anomalous verbs take the same construction, *i. e.*, the subjective, in the past tense also; as मी चाललों I walked; ती शिकली She learnt. The anti-semi-anomalous verbs follow this construction; as तो भात जेवली She ate the rice.

The transitives take the objective and neuter constructions in the past tense; त्यानें गांव जिंकला He conquered the town; त्यानें त्याला मारिलें He struck him.

Note. When the object of a transitive verb is a person, it generally takes the neuter construction; त्यानें राजाला जिंकिलें He conquered the king; त्यानें गांव जिंकला He conquered the town.

☞ There are, however, some exceptions which occur in poetry, and some phrases of long-established usage, over which grammar has no control; thus, मुनिनीं तूं चित्तीं धरिलास The sages contemplated thee; मी स्नान केलों I bathed. In the objective construction the object is usually in the third person. In poetry exceptions occur; as धर्में तूं हरिविलोस Dharma lost thee.

The Voices (वाच्य).

116. Voice is a particular form of the verb, by means of which the relation of the subject of the verb to the action expressed by it is indicated; तो गेला He went.

117. There are two voices, viz., the Active and Passive.

The active voice (कर्तृवाच्य) expresses that the subject is the agent or doer of the action; as मी चालतों I walk.

The passive voice (कर्मणिवाच्य) represents the subject as the object of the action; तो मारला गेला He was killed.

Note. There is not a passive voice in Marâṭhí formed by inflection.

Note (a). Sometimes the verb has an active form but denotes that the subject is affected by the action; as ह्या जात्यांत हरबरे चांगले दळतात The gram is well ground in the mill. This is the peculiarity of the transitive verbs when they are used intransitively. They might be called *Verbs of the Middle Voice.*

(b) Sometimes the verbs have an active form but represent the subject as neither the agent nor the object of the action; as मूल निजतें The child sleeps. These might be called verbs of the *Neuter Voice.*

(c) There are some verbs which represent the subject as neither the agent nor the object of the action, but simply affirm its existence; as मी आहें I am. These are called *Substantive Verbs.*

(*d*) There are other verbs, again, which assert the existence of the subject in a particular condition; तो चांगला दिसतो He looks well, *i. e.*, तो दिसण्यांत चांगला आहे He is good in appearance. These verbs might be called *Neuter-passives*.

(*e*) Some verbs have no subject in the sentence : माझे पोटांत or मला कळमळतें I feel sick; उजाडतें It is daybreak. These verbs are called *Impersonals*.

118. The existing passive form is made up of the past tense of the principal verb, and the various tenses of the verb जाणें To go; तो मारला गेला He was killed. It is not, however, of general use in Maráthí, and occurs chiefly in official correspondence.

CHAPTER X.

CONJUGATION.

(कियापद प्रकिया.)

119. The way in which the personal-endings or verbal inflections, denoting the person, number, gender, tense, mood, and construction, are combined with the verb, is called conjugation.

120. The verb in the imperative second person singular is called the root (धातु); as कर Do thou; सोड Loose thou.

121. In conjugation the personal-endings are affixed to the root. There are *two* ways in which they are affixed, and hence there are *Two Conjugations*, viz., the *First Conjugation* and the *Second Conjugation*.

In the First Conjugation, the personal-endings are affixed to the root, *without modifying it*; as मर To die + तो = मरतो He dies.

In the Second Conjugation, the *root is modified*, before affixing the personal endings, by substituting इ for its final vowel; सोड To loose + इ = सोडि + तो = सोडितो He looses.

The form which the verb assumes before the personal-endings is called the base (पद).

Note. In the Konkaṇ, the इ is scarcely ever heard; as करनो for करितो : in the Dakhan, on the other hand, the vulgar affix it even to verbs of the first conjugation.

122. The verbs are thus arranged under the two conjugations :—

I. Verbs of the First Conjugation.

(1) All intransitive verbs; चाल + तो = चालतो He walks.

(2) All anomalous verbs; पढ + तो = पढतो He learns.

(3) All semi-anomalous verbs; माग + तो = मागतो He asks.

(4) All potential verbs, whether transitive or intransitive; चालव + तें = चालवतें I can walk.

(5) All verbs ending in ह (except the word लोह 'To write) follow this conjugation *in the present tense only;* पाह + तो = पाहतो He sees.

(6) All monosyllabic words follow this conjugation, only, *in the present tense;* as दे give + तो = देतो He gives.

II. Verbs of the Second Conjugation.

(1) All transitive verbs, excepting those specified under the first conjugation; as सोड loose + इ + तो = सोडितो He looses.

(2) The intransitive verbs in ह, and the monosyllabic verbs, whether transitive or intransitive, follow this conjugation *in the past and future enses only;* as पाहा + इ + लें = पाहिलें He saw; जा + ईन = जाईन I shall go; राहा + ईन = राहीन I shall remain.

123. The verbs of both the conjugations have the *same personal. endings in the present tense;* as सोडि + तो = सोडितो He looses; सुट + तो = सुटतो He gets loose : they have, however, different inflections in the past and future tenses.

124. The following is a table of the personal-endings :—

INDICATIVE MOOD.

Present Tense.

1st Conjugation.   *2nd Conjugation.*

Singular.   Plural.

1. तों m. त्यें or तें f. लों or तें n.   तों m. f. n.
2. तोस m. त्येस or तेस, or तीस f. तेंस n.   ता m. f. n.
3. तो m. स्ये, ते, तो f. तें n.   तात m. f. n.

Past Tense.

Kartari Prayoga.   *Karmaṇi Prayoga.*

Sing.   Plu.   Sing.   Plu.

1. लों m. लें f. लों or लें n.   लों m. f. n.   1. ⎫
2. लास m. लीस f. लेंस n.   ला m. f. n.   2. ⎬ ला m. ली f. लें n. लेम. ह्या f. लीं n.
3. ला m. ली f. लें n.   लेम. ह्या f. लीं n.   3. ⎭

Bhávi Prayoga.

1. ⎫
2. ⎬ लें
3. ⎭

Past Habitual Tense.

Sing.   Plu.   Sing.   Plu.

1. एं m. f. n.   ऊं m. f. n.   1. ईं   ऊं
2. एस or अस m. f. n.   आं m. f. n.   2. ईस   आं
3. ए m. f. n.   अन m. f. n.   3. ई   ईत

Future Tense.

Sing.   Plu.   Sing.   Plu.

1. एन m. f. n.   ऊं m. f. n.   1. ईन m. f. n.   ऊं m. f. n.
2. सोल or ह्रोल m. f. n.   आल ,,   2. सील or ह्रोल ,,   आल ,,
3. एल m. f. n.   तील ,,   3. ईल ,,   तोल ,,

(70)

CONDITIONAL MOOD.

PRESENT TENSE.

Singular.	Plural.
1. तों m. तें f. तों or तें n.	तों m. f. n.
2. तास m. तीस f. तेंस n.	ता m. f. n.
3. ता m. ती f. तें n.	ते m. त्या f. तीं n.

SUBJUNCTIVE MOOD.

PRESENT TENSE.

Kartari Prayoga. *Karmaṇi Prayoga.*

Singular.　　Singular.

1. आवा m. -वी f. -वें n.　1. ⎫
2. आवास m. -वीस f. -वेंस n.　2. ⎬ आदा m. -वी f. -वें n.
3. आवा m. -वी f. -वें n.　3. ⎭

Plural.　　Plural.

1. आवें m. -व्या f. -वीं n.　1. ⎫
2. आवेत m. -व्यात f. -वींत n.　2. ⎬ आवे m. -व्या f. -वीं n.
3. आवे m. -व्या f. -वीं n.　3. ⎭

Bhávi Prayoga.

Singular.　Plural.

1. ⎫　　1. ⎫
2. ⎬ आवें　2. ⎬ आवें
3. ⎭　　3. ⎭

IMPERATIVE MOOD.

PRESENT TENSE.

Singular.	Plural.
1. ऊं	1. ऊं
2. अ	2. आ
3. ओ or ऊ	3. ओत or ऊव

INFINITIVE MOOD.

Present Tense.

ऊं

PARTICIPLES.

Present त, ता, तांना
Past ला, लेला
Pluperfect ऊन
Future णार

125. OBSERVATIONS.

(1) The tenses can be formed by affixing the personal-endings to the base.

The base of the verb of the first conjugation does not differ from the verbal root as regards the final vowel; that of the verb of the second conjugation is formed by substituting ई for the final vowel of the verbal root. When the personal-endings begin with a vowel, the Rules of Combination mentioned in the 24th section operate here: सोडी + अवें = सोडावें Should loose; सोडी + आ = सोडा Loose.

Exc. In monosyllabic verbs, the final इ or ए is changed to या in the second plural of the imperative mood: पी + आ = प्या Drink घे + आ = घ्या Take. The third personal forms of the same mood take वो instead of ओ; as घे + ओ = घेवो Let him take; पी + ओत = पिवोत Let them drink.

(2) On a careful consideration of the personal-endings the student will not fail to notice that they are identical, to a great extent, with the third personal pronoun तो. (See Derivations.)

(3) The past forms indicate plainly the same origin as the present forms. The past forms could be produced from the present forms by substituting ल for त; as चालतों I walk; चाललों I walked.

(72)

(4) The past habitual and future forms are distinct for each conjugation.

(5) The conditional, the subjunctive, the imperative, and the infinitive have forms only for the present tense; the indicative alone is conjugated in all the four tenses. Besides these simple tenses, the verbs have Compound Tenses. (See Chap. XII.)

PARADIGMAS.
INDICATIVE MOOD.
PRESENT TENSE.

1st Conjugation.
I get loose *or* am getting loose.

Sing.	Plu.
1. मी सुटतों-तें-तों	आम्ही सुटतों
2. तूं सुटतोस-तीस-तेंस	तुम्ही सुटतां
3. { तो सुटतो / ती सुटती / तें सुटतें	{ ते / त्या / तीं } सुटतात

2nd Conjugation.
I loose *or* am loosing.

Sing.	Plu.
1. मी सोडितों-तें-तों	आम्ही सोडितों
2. तूं सोडितोस-तीस-तेंस	तुम्ही सोडितां
3. { तो सोडितो / ती सोडिती / तें सोडितें	{ ते / त्या / तीं } सोडितात

PAST TENSE.

Kartari Prayoga.
I got loose.

Sing.	Plu.
1. मी सुटलों-लें-लों	आम्ही सुटलों
2. तूं सुटलास-लीस-लेंस	तुम्ही सुटलां
3. { तो सुटला / ती सुटली / तें सुटलें	{ ते सुटले / त्या सुटल्या / तीं सुटलीं }

Karmaṇi Prayoga.
I loosed (him.)

Sing.	Plu.
1. मीं or म्यां or आम्हीं	(तो) सोडिला
2. तूं or त्वां or तुम्हीं	(ती) सोडिली
3. { त्यानें / तिनें / त्यानें } or त्यांनीं	(तें) सोडिलें / (ते) सोडिले / (त्या) सोडिल्या / (तीं) सोडिलीं

Bhávi Prayoga.
I loosed (him).

Sing.	Plu.
1. मीं or म्यां or आम्हीं	
2. तूं or त्वां or तुम्हीं	} सोडिलें
3. { त्यानें / तिनें } or त्यांनीं	

Past Habitual Tense.

1st Conjugation.
I was in the habit of getting loose.

Sing.	Plu.
1. मीं सुटें	1. आम्ही सुटूं
2. तूं सुटेस or सुटस	2. तुम्ही सुटां
3. तो, ती, तें सुटे	3. ने, त्या, नीं, सुटत

2nd Conjugation.
I was wont to loose.

Sing.	Plu.
1. मीं सोडीं	1. आम्ही सोडूं
2. तूं सोडीस	2. तुम्ही सोडां
3. तो, ती, तें सोडी	3. ने, त्या, नीं सोडीत

Future Tense.

1st Conjugation.
I shall get loose.

Sing.	Plu.
1. मीं सुटेन	आम्ही सुटूं
2. तूं सुटसोल	तुम्ही सुटाल
3. तो, ती, तें सुटेल	ने, त्या, तीं सुटतोल

2nd Conjugation.
I shall loose.

Sing.	Plu.
1. मीं सोडीन	1. आम्ही सोडूं
2. तूं सोडिसील	2. तुम्ही सोडाल
3. तो, ती तें सोडील	3. ने, त्या, तीं सोडितील

CONDITIONAL MOOD.

Present Tense.

1st Conjugation.
Were I to get loose, *or* I should get loose.

Sing.	Plu.
1. मीं सुटतों-तें-तीं	1. आम्ही सुटतों
2. तूं सुटतास-तीस-तसें	2. तुम्ही सुटना
3. { तो सुटता / ती सुटती / तें सुटतें	3. { ते सुटते / त्या सुटत्या / तीं सुटतीं

2nd Conjugation.
Were I to loose, *or* I should loose.

Sing.	Plu.
1. मीं सोडितों-तें-तीं	1. आम्ही सोडितों
2. तूं सोडितास-तीस-तेंस	2. तुम्ही सोडिना
3. { तो सोडिता / ती सोडिती / तें सोडितें	3. { ते सोडिते / त्या सोडिल्या / तीं सोडितीं

SUBJUNCTIVE MOOD.

Kartari Prayoga.
1st Conjugation.
I may *or* should get loose.

Sing.	Plu.
1. मीं सुटावा-वी-वें	1. आम्ही सुटावे-व्या-वीं
2. तूं सुटावास-वीस-वेंस	2. तुम्ही सुटावेत-व्यात-वींत
3. { तो सुटावा / ती सुटावी / तें सुटावें	3. { ते सुटवे / त्या सुटाव्या / तीं सुटावीं

Karmani Prayoga.
2nd Conjugation.
I may *or* should loose.

Sing. Plu.	
1. म्यां or आम्हीं	सोडावा-वी-वें Sing.
2. तूं, त्वां or तुह्मीं	सोडावे-व्या-वीं Plu.
3. त्यानें-तिनें-त्यानें or त्यांनीं	

10 *m a*

(74)

Bhávi Prayoga.

I may *or* should get loose. | I may *or* should loose.

Sing.   Plu. | Sing.   Plu.

1. मीं or म्यां or आम्हीं
2. नूं or त्वां or तुम्हीं
   त्यानें
3. तिनें
   त्यानें
} सुटावें

1. म्यां
2. नूं, त्वां
3. त्यानें,
   तिनें, त्यानें
} सोडावें

1. आम्हीं
2. तुम्हीं
3. त्यांनीं
} सोडावें

IMPERATIVE MOOD.

Let me get loose.   Let me loose.

Sing.   Plu. | Sing.   Plu.

1. मीं सुटूं   1. आम्ही सुटूं
2. तूं सूट   2. तुह्मी सुटा
3. { तो
     तो
     तें } सुटो   3. { ने
                           त्यां
                           तीं } सुटोत

1. मी सोडूं   1. आम्ही सोडूं
2. नूं सोड   2. तुम्ही सोडा
3. तो, ती, तें सोडो   3. ते, त्या, तीं सोडोत

INFINITIVE MOOD.

सुटूं To get loose.   सोडूं To loose.

PARTICIPLES.

Present Tense.

सुटत-तां-तांना Getting loose.   सोडीत-तां-तांना Loosing.

Past Tense.

सुटला-लो-लें Got loose.   सोडिला-लो-लें Loosed.

Pluperfect Tense.

सुटून Having got loose.   सोडून Having loosed.

Future Tense.

सुटणार About to get loose.   सोडणार About to loose.

SUPINE.

सुटावें-व्यास-व्याचें To get loose.   सोडावें-व्यास-व्याचें To loose.

GERUND.

सुटणें Getting loose.   सोडणें Loosing.

CHAPTER XI.

CONJUGATION—*continued*.

The Potential Verb.

(शक्य क्रियापद.)

126. The potential verb expresses the ability of the agent to do the action denoted by it; माझ्यानें करवतें I can do it.

It is formed by adding व to the root; as चालणें to walk, चालवणें to be able to walk. Monosyllabic verbs, and verbs ending in ह, double the व; खाणें to eat, खाववणें to be able to eat; पाहणें to see, पाहववणें to be able to see.

Note. लिहिणें is an exception, since it takes only one ह; as लिहवणें to be able to write.

127. The potential verb follows the first conjugation in all the tenses, and is rarely conjugated in any other mood than the indicative.

128. It differs, however, very widely from the other verbs in the matter of the Prayogas, and the following particulars are important:—

(1) The subject of the potential verb is always in an oblique case, viz., either the dative, or the genitive instrumental; मला or माझ्यानें जाववतें I can go.

Note. मला is colloquially used, and माझ्यानें classically.

(2) It always takes the *Bhávi* construction, unless it has an un-inflected object, as in त्याच्यानें आंबा खाववला He could eat the mango. The transitive verb takes this construction, also, in the present tense; रामाला पोथी वाचवती Rámá can read the book.

Note. For the potential verbs may be substituted other forms: (1) the present participle तां, or the dative of the supine is used with the different parts of the verb येणें to come; मला लिहितां येतें I can write; and (2) the infinitive mood is used with the various tenses of the verb शकणें to be able; मी करूं शकतों I can do it. The latter form is neither elegant nor idiomatic.

Potential Verb.

First Conjugation.

INDICATIVE MOOD.

Present Tense.

I can get loose (intr. v.) *and* I can loose (tr. v.)

Bhávi Prayoga.

Sing.		Plu.	
1. माझ्यानें or मला	सुटवतें (intr. v.) सोडवनें (tr. v.)	1. आमच्यानें or आह्माला	सुटवनें (intr. v.) सोडवनें (tr. v.)
2. तुझ्यानें or तुला		2. तुमच्यानें or तुह्मालां	
3. त्याच्यानें or त्याला m. n. तिच्यानें or तिला f.		3. त्याच्यानें or त्यांला	

Karmaṇi Prayoga.

I can loose.

Sing.		Plu.	
1. माझ्यानें or मला	सोडवतोm. -ती f. -तें n. सोडवतान m.f.n.Plu.	1. आमच्यानें or आह्माला	सोडवतो m. -ती f. -तें n. Sing. सोडवनान Plu.
2. तुझ्यानें or तुला		2. तुमच्यानें or तुह्माला	
3. त्याच्यानें or त्याला m. n. तिच्यानें or तिला f.		3. त्याच्यानें or त्यांला	

Past Tense.

Bhávi Prayoga.

I could get loose (intr. v.) *and* I could loose (tr. v.)

Sing.		Plu.	
1. माझ्यानें or मला	सुटवलें (intr.v.) सोडवलें (tr. v.)	1. आमच्यानें or आह्माला	सुटवलें (intr. v.) सोडवलें (tr. v.)
2. तुझ्यानें or तुला		2. तुमच्यानें or तुह्माला	
3. त्याच्यानें or त्याला m. n. तिच्यानें or निला f.		3. त्याच्यानें or त्यांला	

Past Habitual Tense.

Sing.		Plu.	
1. 2. 3. } माझ्यानें or मला सुटवे &c., &c. सोडवे	(intr.v.) (tr. v.)	1. 2. 3. } आमच्यानें or आह्माला सुटवे &c., &c. सोडवे	(intr. v.) (tr. v.)

Future Tense.

Bhávi Prayoga.

I shall be able to get loose (intr. v.) *and* I shall be able to loose (tr. v.).

Sing.

1. माझ्यानें or मला
2. तुझ्यानें or तुला
3. त्याच्यानें or त्याला
   m. n. तिच्यानें or
   निला f.

} सुटवेल (intr. v.) सोडवेल (tr. v.)

Plu.

1. आमच्यानें or आम्हाला
2. तुमच्यानें or तुम्हाला
3. त्याच्यानें or त्याला

} सुटवेल (intr. v.) सोडवेल (tr.v.)

Participles.

Present. { सुटवन-ता-तांना (intr. v.) Capable of getting loose.
सोडवन-ता-तांना (tr. v.) Able to loose.

Past. सोडवला-ली-लें Sing.; सोडवले-ह्या-लीं Plu. (tr. v.)

Future. { सुटवणार (intr. v.) About to be able to get loose.
सोडवणार (tr. v.) About to be able to loose.

The Causal Verb.

(प्रयोज्य क्रियापद.)

129. Causal verbs denote the doing of an act by the agent through the instrumentality of another; म्यां त्याच्याकडून करविलें I got it done by him.

130. The causal verb is formed by adding वि to the root of the transitive verb; मारणें to kill, मारविणें to cause to kill.

Monosyllabic roots and those ending in ह take a double व; खाणें to eat, खावविणें to cause to eat; लिहिणें to write, लिहवविणें to cause to write.

Note. When वि is affixed to intransitive verbs, they become transitive, and not causal; as निजणें to sleep, निजविणें to put to sleep.

131. The causals, being transitives, follow the second conjugation. They are never irregularly conjugated.

Note. The anomalous verbs, the irregular verbs, &c., all follow the same conjugation; शिकणें to teach, त्यानें शिकविलें he taught, *not* नों शिकविला; करविणें to cause to do, कर्रविलें caused to do, and *not* केलर्विलें.

Note. Some affix इव instead of वि to the root to make up the causal verb; as सोडिवणें To cause to loose. The imperative of both the forms is alike in the singular number and second person; as सोडीव Do thou cause to loose.

The following are the tenses of the causal verb:—

Present Tense. मी सोडवितों I cause to loose.
Past Tense. म्यां सोडविलें I caused to loose.
Past Habitual. मी सोडवीं I used to cause to loose.
Future Tense. मी सोडवीन I shall cause to loose.

Note. For further observations on the causal verbs see the chapters on Derivation.

THE IRREGULAR VERB.

(अनियमित क्रियापद.)

132. Several verbs, both transitive and intransitive, are irregularly conjugated in the past tense, and the following is a list of them. They are arranged in three groups; 1st, those which change the final vowel of the root to आ; 2ndly, those which have a past tense formed from another root; and 3rdly, those which modify the root by means of consonants and semivowels.

(1) Roots which substitute आ :—

Root.		Past Tense.
नीघ	Go out.	निघाला
पळ	Flee.	पळाला
झण	Say.	झणाला or झटलें
रीघ	Penetrate by force.	रिघाला
हींव	Be cold.	हिंवाला

Note.—The above verbs have *only the specified* forms for the past tense.

झिर	Soak into.	झिराला	or	झिरला
ढळ	Slip aside.	ढळाला	or	ढळला
निड	Crack.	निडाला	or	निडला
निभ	Get out of.	निभाला	or	निभला
भिज	Be wetted.	भिजाला	or	भिजला
मुर	Be absorbed.	मुराला	or	मुरला

Note. The second past form is in general use.

उड	Fly.	उडाला	or	उडला
दड	Lie hid.	दडाला	or	दडला
निम	Cease.	निमाला	or	निमला
निव	Cool.	निवाला	or	निवला
बुड	Sink.	बुडाला	or	बुडला
मिळ	Meet with.	मिळाला	or	मिळला
विर	Melt.	विराला	or	विरला

Note. The first past form is in general use.

उभ	Cease for a time.	उभाला	or	उभला
खिज	Grate.	खिजाला	or	खिजला
गळ	Leak.	गळाला	or	गळला
जळ	Burn.	जळाला	or	जळला
झिज	Wear away.	झिजाला	or	झिजला
दब	Yield or give way.	दबाला	or	दबला
दिप	Be dazzled.	दिपाला	or	दिपला
बुज	Start.	बुजाला	or	बुजला
बुझ	Understand.	बुझाला	or	बुझला
रिझ	Be delighted with.	रिझाला	or	रिझला
लप	Lie hid.	लपाला	or	लपला
विझ	Be extinguished.	विझाला	or	विझला

Note. Both the forms are equally used.

(2) Verbs that have a past tense formed from another root.

(80)

Root.		Past Tense.
जा	Go	गेला
ये	Come	आला
हो	Become	झाला

(3) Verbs which substitute different consonants and vowels for some of the letters of the root in order to make up the past tense :—

गा	Sing	गाइलें or गालें
ध्या	Meditate	ध्याइलें or ध्यालें
मा	Hold	माइलें or मालें
घे	Take	घेतलें
पी	Drink	प्यालें
भू	Wash	भुतलें
भी	Fear	भ्यालें
वी	Bear	व्यालें
ले	Wear	ल्यालें
दे	Give	दिलें
बघ	See	बघितलें
माग	Ask	मागितलें
सांग	Tell	सांगितलें
खण	Dig	खणलें or खंटलें
म्हण	Say	म्हटलें
हाण	Slay	हाटलें
घाल	Put	घातलें
कर	Do	केलें
मर	Die	मेलें
खा	Eat	खाल्लें

The Irregular Verbs are thus conjugated in the various tenses :—

कर Do.

मी करितों	I do	Present Tense.
मीं or म्यां केलें	I did	Past Tense.
तूं or त्वां केलें	Thou didst	,,

त्यानें केलें	He did.	—Past Tense.
आम्हीं केलें	We did.	,,
तुम्हीं केलें	You did.	,,
त्यानीं केलें	They did.	,,
मी करीन	I shall do.	— Future Tense.
तूं करशील	Thou shalt do.	,,
तो करील	He shall do.	,,
मी जातों	I go.	— Present Tense.
मी गेलों	I went.	— Past Tense.
तूं गेलास	Thou wentest.	,,
तो गेला	He went.	,,
आम्हीं गेलों	We went.	,,
तुम्हीं गेला	You went.	,,
ते गेले	They went.	,,
मी जाईन	I shall go.	— Future Tense.
तूं जाशील	Thou shalt go, &c. &c.	

CONJUGATION OF THE ANOMALOUS VERBS.

133. The Anomalous Verbs, *though transitive in sense*, are entirely conjugated like the intransitives in the First Conjugation. Though they take an object in the past tense, they follow the subjective or *Kartari* construction. Thus,—

मी पढतों I study (and not पढितों).

मी पोथी पढलों I studied a book (and not म्यां पोथी पढली).

मी पढेन I shall study (and not पढीन).

मी त्याला विसरलों I forgot him (and not म्यां त्याला विसरलें).

11 *m a*

(82)

134. The following are the anomalous verbs in the language :—

आचरणें	To practise.	म्हणणें	To say.
आठवणें	To remember.	विणें	To bring forth.
ओकणें	To vomit.	समजणें	To understand.
चावणें	To bite.	लागणें	To affect.
जेवणें	To dine.	शिंकरणें	To blow the nose.
झोंबणें	To seize hold of.	स्मरणें	To remember.
थुंकणें	To spit.	लेणें	To put on.
नेसणें	To gird on.	विसरणें	To forget.
पढणें	To study.	शिवणें	To touch.
पांघरणें	To clothe.	पसवणें	To foal.
पावणें	To obtain.	प्रसवणें	To bring forth.
पिणें	To drink.	मुकणें	To lose.
पोहणें	To swim.	नरणें	To pass over.
बोलणें	To tell.		

CONJUGATION OF THE SUBSTANTIVE VERBS.

135. The substantive verbs are verbs that denote existence; they are आहे, होय To be, or to be in a particular state; होणें To become, or to enter into a particular state of being.

Note. (1) आहे denotes simple existence, in a general or particular state; and is used in relation to both persons and qualities.

(2) होय is used in relation to qualities only.

(3) असणें denotes continuance in a particular state or an habitual state of existence. But (4) होणें differs from the above forms in this, that it expresses *entrance*

into a new state, or the acquisition of a new property. Besides this usual sense of होणें To become, it signifies, also—

a. To come to pass; त्यान्नीं भेट झाली His meeting has taken place = I have met him.

b. In the past and future it expresses the completion of an action; त्यान्चें जेवण झालें His dinner is done.

c. In union with other verbs, its senses vary; as येते व्हा, जाने व्हा, &c., implying begin and go through with it.

d. It has the sense of an adverb; as तो होऊन जर मुलगी द्यायास आला तर करीन If he of himself should offer his daughter in marriage, then I will wed her. Of these verbs, the verbs असणें and होणें are regularly conjugated in *all* the moods and tenses and, being intransitive verbs, fall under the first conjugation; the rest are defective in tense-forms.

136. Each of these substantive verbs has a negative form; thus—

मी आहें I am, मी नाहीं I am not.
मी होय „   मी नव्हें „
मी असतों I usually am, मी नसतों I usually am not.
मी होतों I become, मी होत नाहीं I do not become.

Note. The verb होणें, To become, has not a simple negative form.

Indicative Mood.

Present Tense.

137. आहें To be.

Singular.	Plural.
1. मी आहें I am.	आम्ही आहों We are.
2. तूं आहेस Thou art.	तुम्ही आहा Ye are.
3. तो, ती, ते आहे He, She or It is.	ते, त्या, तीं आहेत They are.

138. होय To be.

Singular.	Plural.
1. मी होय I am.	आम्ही व्हों We are.
2. तूं होस Thou art.	तुम्ही व्हा Ye are.
3. तो, ती, ते होय He, She, or It is.	ते, त्या, तीं होत They are.

Past Tense.

Singular.	Plural.
1. मी होतों m. n होतें f. I was.	आम्ही होतों We were.
2. तूं होतास m. होतीस f. होतेंस n. Thou wast.	तुम्ही होतां Ye were.
3. तो होता m. ती होती f. तें होतें n. He, She, It was.	ते होते m. त्या होत्या f. तीं होतीं n. They were.

Note. Both these verbs have no other forms, and the other tenses, which are usually joined to them, belong to one or other of the succeeding verbs.

139. असणें To be usually.

INDICATIVE MOOD.

Present Tense.

Singular.	Plural.
1. मां असतों m. तें f. तों n. I usually am.	आह्मी असतों m. f. n.
2. तूं असतोस m. तीस f. तेंस n.	तुह्मी असतां ,,
3. तो, तो, तें असतो m. ती f. तें n.	ते, त्या, तीं असतात ,,

Past Tense.

Singular.	Plural.
1. मी असें I usually was, *or* was in the habit of being.	आम्ही असूं.
2. तूं असस.	तुम्ही असां.
3. तो, ती, तें असे.	ते, त्या, तीं असत.

Future Tense.

Singular.	Plural.
1. मी असेन I shall be	आम्ही असूं.
2. तूं अससील or शील.	तुम्ही असाल.
3. तो, ती, तें असेल.	ते, त्या, तीं असतील.

Conditional Mood.

Present Tense.

Singular.	Plural.
1. मीं असतों m. न, तें. f. Were I, *or* I would be, Had I been, *or* I would have been.	आम्ही असतों m. f. n. तुम्ही असतां m. f. n.
2. तूं असतास m. तीस f. तेंस n.	ते, त्या, तीं असते m.
3. तो, ती, तें असता m. ती f. तें n.	त्या f. तीं n.

Past Tense.

Singular.	Plural.
1. मीं असलों m. लें f. लों n. Should I be.	आम्हीं असलों m. f. n.
2. तूं असलास m. लीस f. लेंस n.	तुम्ही असला m. f. n.
3. तो असला m. ली f. लें n.	ते, त्या, तीं असले m, ह्या f. लीं n.

Future.

Singular.	Plural.
1. मी असेन I may (perhaps) be, *or* I may (perhaps) have been.	1. आम्ही असूं.
2. तूं अससील or शील.	2. तुम्ही असाल.
3. तो, तो, तें असेल.	3. ते, त्या, तीं असतील.

Subjunctive Mood.

Kartari Prayoga.

Singular.	Plural.
1. मीं असावा m. वी f. वें n. I may, can, could, would, *or* should be, *or* have been.	आह्मी असावे m. व्या f. वीं n.
2. तूं असावास m. वीस f. वेंस n.	तुह्मी असावे m. व्यात f. बीत n.
3. तो, तो नें असावा m. वी f. वें n.	ते, त्या, तीं असावे m. व्या f. वीं n.

Bhávi Prayoga.

Singular.	Plural.
1. म्यां असावें I should be.	आम्हीं असावें.
2. त्वां असावें.	तुह्मीं असावें.
3. त्यानें, निनें, त्यानें असावें.	त्यांनीं असावें.

Imperative Mood.

Singular.	Plural.
1. मी असूं Let me be, *i. e.*, continue.	आह्मीं असूं.
2. तूं अस or ऐस.	तुह्मीं असा.
3. तो, ती, तें असो.	ते, त्या, तीं असोत

Infinitive Mood.

असूं To be usually, *or* continue to be.

Participles.

Present असत, असंतां, असतांना Being.

Supines.

Dat. असायास -याला To be, *i. e.*, continue.
Gen. असायाचें Is to be.

Gerund.

असणें -ण्याला -ण्याचें To be, or being, &c.

140. The verb होणें To become, is thus conjugated :—

Indicative Mood.

Present Tense.

Singular.	Plural.
1. मी होतों m. तें f. तों n. I become.	आह्मीं होतों m. f. n.
2. तूं होतास m. तेस f. तेंस n.	तुह्मीं होतां m. f. n.
3. तो, ती, तें होतो m. ने f. नें n.	ते, त्या, नीं होतात m. f. n.

Past Tense.

Singular.	Plural.
1. मीं झालों m. n. लें f. I became.	आम्ही झालों m. f. n.
2. तूं झालास m. लीस f. लेंस n.	तुम्ही झालां m. f. n.
3. तो, ती, तें झाला-लि-लें.	ते, त्या, तीं झाले-ल्या-लीं.

Past Habitual Tense.

Singular.	Plural.
1. मी होंई I was wont to become.	आम्ही होऊं.
2. तूं होईस or होस.	तुम्ही व्हा.
3. तो, ती, तें होंई.	ते, त्या, तीं होईत or होन.

Future Tense.

Singular.	Plural.
1. मी होईन I shall become, *or* may perhaps become.	आम्ही होऊं.
2. तूं होसील.	तुम्ही व्हाल.
3. तो, ती, तें होईल.	ते, त्या, तीं होतील.

Conditional Mood.

Singular मी होतों Were I to become, *or* I would become *or* have become. It is conjugated like the indicative होतों I was.

Subjunctive Mood.

Singular. m. f. n.	Plural. m. f. n.
1. मी व्हावा-वी-वें. I may become.	आम्ही व्हावे-व्या-वीं.
2. तूं व्हावास-वीस-वेंस.	तुम्ही व्हावेत-व्यात-वींत.
3. तो, ती, तें व्हावा-वी-वें.	ते, त्या, तीं व्हावे-व्हाव्या-व्हावीं

Note. The above are the *Kartari* forms, and the *Bhávi Prayoga* forms are म्यां व्हावें I should become, &c.

IMPERATIVE MOOD.

Singular.	Plural.
1. मीं होंडं Let me become.	आह्मी होडं.
2. तूं हो.	तुम्ही व्हा.
3. तो, ती, तें होवो -ऊ.	ते, त्या, तीं होवोत-ऊन.

INFINITIVE MOOD.

होंडं To become.

PARTICIPLES.

Present, होत, होता, होतांना Becoming.
Past, झाला-लो-लें, लें-ल्या-लीं, झालेला-लेलो, &c. Become.
Pluperfect, होऊन Having become.
Future, होणार About to become.

SUPINE.

Dat. व्हावयास-ला, व्हायास-ला To become.
Gen. व्हावयाचें Is to become.

GERUND.

होणें, &c. Becoming.

NEGATIVE VERBS.

141. नाहीं is the negative of आहे, and is used to negate both existence and qualities. It is conjugated as follows:—

Singular.	Plural.
1. मी नाहीं I am not.	आम्ही नाहीं
2. तूं नाहींस	तुम्ही नाहीं
3. तो, ती, तें नाहीं	ते, त्या, तीं नाहींत

142. नव्हें is the negative of होय, and is used principally to negate qualities.

Singular.	Plural.
1. मी नव्हें I am not.	आम्ही नव्हों, नव्हे
2. तूं नव्हेस, नव्हस	तुम्ही नव्हा, नव्हेत
3. तो, ती, तें नव्हे	ते, त्या, तीं नव्हेत or नव्हत

143. नव्हतों is the negative form of होतों, and is conjugated as follows :—

Singular.	Plural.
1. मी नव्हतों m. तें f. तों n. I was not.	आम्ही नव्हतों m. f. n.
2. तूं नव्हतास m. -तीस f. तेंस n.	तुम्ही नव्हता m. f. n.
3. तो, ती, तें नव्हता-ती-तें	ते, त्या तीं, नव्हते-न्या-तीं

144. नसणें *The Negative form of* असणें.

Present Ind. मी नसतों m. -तें f. -तीं n. I am not in the habit of being.

Past Ind. मी नसें m. f. n. I was not in the habit of being.

Future Ind. मी नसेन m. f. n. I shall not usually be.

Pres. Cond. मी नसतों m. Were I not, Had I not been.

Past Cond. मी नसलों m. Should I not be.

Subjunctive म्यां नसावें or असूं नये I should not be.

Imp. 2nd Sing. असूं नको Do not continue to be ; Plu. असूं नका Do not continue to be.

Imp. 3rd Sing. नसो Let him not be ; Plu. नसोत Let them not be.

Supine नसायास Not to continue to be.

Participle नसतां Not being.

Gerund नसणें Not to continue to be.

145. *Negative forms of* होणें.

Present मी होत नाहीं I am not becoming.

तूं होत नाहींस Thou art not becoming, &c.

Past Ind. मी न झालों, or, more commonly, झालों नाहीं I did not become.

Past Habit. मी न होईं, or, more commonly, हेईना I was not wont to become.

Pluperfect मी झालों नव्हतों I had not become.

Future Ind. मी न होईन, or, more commonly, होणार नाहीं I shall not become.

Pres. Cond. मी न होतों Were I not to become.

Pres. Subj. म्यां न व्हावें, or, more frequently, होऊं नये I should not become.

Imp. 2nd Pers. Sing. होऊं नको (Plu. होऊं नका) Do not become.

Imp. 3rd Pers. Sing. न होवो (Plu. न होवोत) Let him not become.

Supine नव्हायास Not to become.

Past Participle न होतां Not becoming.

Gerund न होणें Not to become.

DEFECTIVE VERBS (गौण क्रियापद).

146. The defectives are पाहिजे It is wanted, नको It is not wanted, नलगे It is not necessary, and नये It is not proper; besides there are the substantive verbs, आहे and होय:—

(1) पाहिजे is thus conjugated.

INDICATIVE MOOD.

Kartari Prayoga.

Singular.   Plural.

मी पाहिजे I am wanted.   आम्ही पाहिजे.

तूं पाहिजे or पाहिजेस Thou art wanted.   तुम्ही पाहिजे.

तो, ती, तें पाहिजे He, She, or It is wanted.   ते, त्या, तीं पाहिजेत.

Note. पाहिजेल is, sometimes, used for पाहिजे in the future tense: मला तो पाहिजे or पाहिजेल.

The *Past tense* is formed with होणें; as मला ती गाई पाहिजे होती I wanted that cow. पाहिजेन is, sometimes, used in such combinations; as तुला तें पाहिजेत or पाहिजे असेल तर घे Take it if you should want it.

(2) नको is the opposite of पाहिजे; मला द्रव्य नको I do not want riches. It is thus conjugated :—

Singular.	Plural.
मी नको I am not wanted.	आम्ही नको.
तूं नको Thou art not wanted.	तुम्ही नको.
तो, ती, तें नको He, She, or It is not wanted.	ते, त्या, तीं नकात.

Note. When नको is used as a negative auxiliary, its second person plural is नका; thus तुम्ही करूं नका Do not do it.

(3) नये is used only as an auxiliary, and is thus conjugated :—

Singular.	Plural.
मीं or म्यां करूं नये I should not do it.	आम्हीं करूं नये.
तूं or त्वां करूं नये Thou shouldst not do it.	तुम्हीं करूं नये.
त्यानें, तिनें करूं नये He, She, or It should not do it.	त्यानीं करूं नये.

(4) नलगे (न लागणें) is used generally with the 3rd person singular noun, the gerund, or the nominative supine; तिला तुझें वस्त्र नलगे She does not want your dress; मला जावें नलगे It is not necessary for me to go; तीस बोध करणें नलगे It is not necessary to teach her. Its plural form is नलगेत.

COMPOUND VERBS (संयुक्त क्रियापद).

147. There are comparatively few simple verbs in Maráthí, and their deficiency is made up by the following methods :—

(1) A verb is combined with a noun; as विश्वास धरणें To believe.
अंगांत घालणें To wear.
सिद्धीस नेणें To finish.
प्रीति करणें To love.

(2) A verb is combined with a participle; as टाकून देणें To cast away.

घेऊन येणें To bring.

साधून घेणें To acquire.

Note. In the two latter examples with ये and घे, the principal act is not in the participle as in the former case, but in the supplemental verbs.

(3) A verb is combined with an adverb; as ठार मारणें To kill.

उत्पन्न करणें To create.

प्रकट करणें To publish.

148. Some of the principal verbs which are thus employed to make up new verbal forms are the following:—

करणें	To make.	मारणें	To beat.
घालणें	To throw.	पावणें	To reach.
धरणें	To lay hold of.	वाटणें	To seem.
ठेवणें	To place.	खाणें	To eat.
देणें	To give.	नेणें	To lead.
टाकणें	To throw away.		

Note. Each of these verbs has its own particular use; thus, to love is प्रीति करणें or ठेवणें with the preposition वर upon, coming after the object: as त्यावर प्रीति केली or ठेविली; but प्रीति धरणें or बाळगणें with the genitive of the object: as याची प्रीति धरली or बाळगली. To wear is अंगांत घालणें, and not ठेवणें or टाकणें.

CHAPTER XII.

COMPOUND TENSES.

149. Compound Tenses are formed by means of the substantive verbs, and the participles, or the simple tenses of the principal verbs.

The substantive verbs and all other verbs which are employed in forming compound tenses are called Auxiliary or helping verbs.

The verbs with which the auxiliary verbs are combined are called principal verbs. Thus, in तो लिहीत असतो He is in the habit of writing, लिहीत is the present participle of the principal verb लिहिणें, and असतो is the third singular present of the auxiliary verb असणें to be.

The compound tenses indicate modifications of time present, past, and future.

THE INDICATIVE MOOD.

150. The indicative mood has three forms for the present tense, five for the past, and five for the future, besides the simple tenses.

Present Tense.

(1) The *Present Imperfect* or *Progressive* is formed of the present participle, and the present tense of the verb to be; तो लिहीत आहे He is writing. It expresses that the action is in a state of progression.

Note.—It also expresses an act that was in progression at a past time; पाखरें येत आहेत जात आहेत असें त्यानें पाहिलें He saw the birds going and coming.

(2) The *Present Imperfect Emphatic* is the present tense with the verb आहे; as तो रडतो आहे He is crying. This form is perhaps a little more emphatic than the former.

Note.—It also denotes an action, whether completed or not, that has been in progress for some time; आज मी लिहितों आहें I am engaged in writing to-day (without being employed in writing at that precise time).

(3) The *Present Habitual* is the present tense formed with the present tense of the verb असणें; as मासे समुद्रांत रहात असतात Fishes live in the sea. It expresses a habit or the usual state of the agent.

Past Tense.

(1) *The Past Imperfect* or *Progressive* is the present participle with the past tense of आहे; इतक्यांत वाघ येत होता At that instant a tiger was approaching. It expresses that an action was in progress at a particular past period.

(2) The *Perfect tense* is formed with the past tense and the present tense of the verb आहे; as त्यानें ग्रंथ केला आहे He has written a book (which book remains to the present day). It expresses an action perfected some time ago, but the consequences of which extend to the present time.

Note. It is occasionally used dramatically for the pluperfect tense; तो चालला आहे इतक्यांत राजा आला As he was going, the king came there. (चालला आहे = चालला होता.)

(3) The *Pluperfect tense* is formed with the past tense and the past tense of the verb आहे; त्यांनीं तिला ताटीवर निजविलें होतें तेव्हां म्यां पाहिलें Just after they had placed her on the bier I saw her; ती थंड झाली होती She had become cold. It expresses an action which was past before some other specified past action.

Note. It sometimes denotes simple past action; मावशीनें माझे वाढदिवशीं ही आंगठी दिली होती My maternal aunt gave me this ring on my birthday; नौका दोरीनें बांधली होती The boat lay tied fast by a rope.

(4) The *Past Habitual* is the present participle and the past habitual tense of असणें; as माला करून तो ब्राह्मण नित्य बसत असे Having erected a temporary watch-tower, that Bráhman was in the daily habit of sitting on it.

(5) The *Continuative Past*, formed of the present participle ending in ता and the past tense of the verb होणें; भूतराष्ट्र बोलता झाला Dritaráshtra began to speak. It expresses the commencement and continuance of an act.

6. The *Dubitative Past*, formed with the past tense of the verb and असेन and असावा; तुझीं मला शिकविलें असेल or असावें You must have taught me. It expresses the probable occurrence of an event in past time.

7. The *Past Prospective* is the future participle and the past tense of the verb होणें; as तुम्हीं माणूस पाठविला नेव्हां मी लिहिणार होतों I

was to write when you sent the man. It expresses the intention of the agent to do some act in the past specified time.

Note. It also expresses the intention of the agent to do a certain act in time past but he did not do it; as मी काल आपणाकडे येणार होतों पण शरीरांत विकृती झाल्यामुळें घरींच राहिलों I was to have called on you yesterday, but having felt unwell I stayed at home. This is the pluperfect prospective.

FUTURE TENSE.

(1) The *Future Imperfect* or *Progressive* is the present participle with असेन; मी बारा वाजतां तुझी वाट पाहत असेन I shall be waiting for you at twelve o'clock. It expresses willingness to continue the performance of a particular act in future time.

Note. It also expresses contingency, present or future; तुझा बाप तुझी वाट पाहत असेल Your father most probably will be (or must be) expecting your return.

(2) The *Future Continuative* is the present participial adjective and the future of होणें; as तो चालता होईल He will begin to go away. It expresses the commencement and continuance of a future act in future time.

(3) The *Present Prospective* is the future participle of the verb with आहे; as काय खेळणार आहां? What are you going to play? It signifies the future accomplishment of an act that has been resolved on.

Note. The chief use of this tense is, by its negative form, to deny what is affirmed in the simple future form; thus असें कसें होईल? How can that be? असें होणार नाहीं That cannot be.

(4) The *Future Future* is the future participle in णार with असेन; तुम्ही याल तेव्हां मी लिहिणार असेन I shall be going to write when you come.

Note. It has also the sense of contingency.

CONDITIONAL MOOD.

PRESENT PROGRESSIVE.

151. This is formed by the present participle and the present conditional of असणें; तो जर काम करीत असता तर असा अनर्थ कशानें घडता?

Had he been employed at his work, how could such an accident have occurred? It expresses the possibility of an action in progress at the specified time, whether present or past.

Present Dubitative.

This is the present participle and असलें; तो जात असला, तर तें काम त्याला सांग Should he be going, then intrust the business to him. It expresses an uncertainty or doubt respecting occurrence of an event in present time.

Past Tense.

This is the past indicative and the present conditional of the verb असणें; तें थोडक्यांत चुकलें, नाहीं तर ती पडली असती It missed by a little, otherwise she would have fallen (she narrowly escaped a fall).

Past Dubitative.

This is the past tense with असलें; मी असी लबाडी केली असली, तर मग मी द्वाड खरा Should I really have been guilty of such roguery, then truly I am a blackguard. It expresses an uncertainty respecting an action, which, if it had ever occurred at all, must now be past.

Future Dubitative.

This is the future participle with असलें; जर तो जाणार असला, तर मला सांग Should he be going then tell me. It expresses an uncertainty respecting an event, which, if it is to occur at all, will occur in future time.

Note. The principal difference between the conditional forms in तों or असतों and असलों is this, that the former do not imply the truth of the conditional proposition, whereas the latter simply indicate a doubt or uncertainty respecting the truth of it. तो मरता or मेला असता Had he died, implies that he is not dead; but तो मेला असला If he should be dead, implies that he may or may not be dead, but the speaker has no knowledge of the fact.

152. SUBJUNCTIVE MOOD.

Past Tense.

This is the present subjunctive with होतें; as त्वां सांगावें होतें You should have told.

Note. Besides the substantive verbs, the subjunctive mood takes other auxiliary verbs. It uses also other verbal forms besides that in आवें.

(1) *Present Tense*; मला चालळें पाहिजे I must walk. (Formed of the past indicative and पाहिजे.)

(2) *Present Tense*; मला चालायाचें पडतें I am under the necessity of walking (Formed of the genitive supine and पडणें.)

(3) *Present Tense*; मला चालावें लागतें I must walk. (Formed of the nominative supine and the neuter singular of लागणें.)

(4) *Present or Future*; मला चालायाचें आहे I must walk, or I have to walk. (Formed of the genitive supine and आहे.)

(1) *Past Tense*; मला चालायाचें पडलें I was under the necessity of walking.

(2) *Past Tense*; मला चालावें लागे It was necessary for me to walk.

(3) *Past Tense*; मला चालळें पाहिजे होतें I should have walked.

(4) *Past Tense*; मला चालायाचें होतें I had to walk.

(1) *Future Tense*; मला चालावयाचें पडेल I should be under the necessity of walking.

(2) *Future Tense*; मला चालावें लागेल It will be necessary for me to walk.

(3) *Future Tense*; मला चालळें पाहिजे I must walk.

153. PARTICIPLES.

Present Participle.

This is formed with the present participle of the verb and the participle असतां or असतानां; as भोज राजा राज्य करीत असतां एका ब्राह्मणानें नवी भूमि साधून ज्ञेत पेरिलें होतें During the reign of Bhoja Rájá, a certain

13 *m a*

Bráhman, having acquired a piece of waste land, sowed it with grain. It expresses the time during which the verbal act takes place.

Past Participle.

This is the past participle with असतां; as तो खालीं भाला असतां स्याची बुद्धि पुनः पूर्ववत् व्हावी Whenever he came down, his disposition would become the same as before. It expresses that the participial act is the occasion of the verbal act.

Note. It expresses, also, a possible conditionality; as उपाय केला असतां दुर्गुण टाकवितां येईल If means be used, it will still be possible to rid him of his bad qualities.

154. COMPOUND NEGATIVE TENSES.

The negative forms of the verbs are formed by joining the negative particles न not, or the negative forms of the substantive verbs, to simple participles; as मी सोडीत नाहीं I am not loosing.

The following are compound negative tenses:—

Present Sing.   1. मी सोडीत नाहीं I am not loosing.
   „   „   2. तूं सोडीत नाहींस Thou art not loosing.
   „   „   3. तो, ती, तें सोडीत नाहीं He, she, or it is not loosing.
   „   *Plu.* 1. आम्ही सोडीत नाहीं We are not loosing.
   „   „   2. तुम्ही सोडीत नाहीं You are not loosing.
   „   „   3. ते, त्या, तीं सोडीत नाहीं They are not loosing.

Past. मी न सोडिलें or मी सोडिलें नाहीं I did not loose.

Past Habitual. मी न सोडीं or सोडींना I was not wont to loose.

Pluperfect. मी सोडलें नव्हतें I had not loosed.

Future. मी न सोडीन or मी सोडणार नाहीं I shall not loose.

Present Conditional. मी न सोडितों Were I not to loose.

Present Subjunctive. म्यां न सोडावें or म्यां सोडूं नये I should not loose.

Imperative 2nd Person Sing. सोडूं नको; *Plu.* सोडूं नका Do not loose

Gerund. न सोडणें Not to loose.

Present Participle. न सोडितां Not loosing.

Note. When there are two forms given of one tense, the latter is more commonly used; as मी सोडणार नाहीं I shall not loose, is preferred to मी न सोडीन, future indicative. Besides नाहीं and नव्हतें, the verb नसणें is used to form the compound negative tenses; as,

Present Indicative. मी सोडीन नसनों m. तें f. तों n.

Note. The first personal forms only have been given here; the rest are formed on the same principle.

Note. Some other auxiliary negative verbs are also employed to form the compound negative tenses, such as नये, नलगे, &c.

155. THE PASSIVE VOICE.

The passive forms are composed of the past participle in ला of the principal verb, and the simple tenses of the verb जाणें to go.

Note. The passive voice is not of general use in Maráthí, although it is freely used in Sanskrit and Prákrit. In the latter languages the verb is inflected to denote the passive relation; thus कृ To do (S.), करोति (S.) Does; क्रियते (S.), करिजेलो Prák. has been done. In the passive voice the agent may or may not be specified; thus, दोऱ्यानें गाई बाभळी गेली The cow was tied with a rope, or रामाकडून गाई दोऱ्यानें बाभळी गेली The cow was tied by Rámá with a rope. The agent of a passive voice is governed by a postposition denoting instrumentality; as कडून, योगानें, करवीं &c. The methods to which natives have resorted to avoid this passive form will be found in the syntax. A native would never say दोऱ्यानें गाई बाभळी गेली, but दोऱ्यानें गाई बाभळी होती The cow was tied with a rope.

Present Indicative.

Singular.	Plural.
1. मी सोडिला जानों m -ली जानें f. -लें जानों n. I am loosed.	1. आम्ही सोडिले जानों m. -ल्या जानों f. -लीं जानों n. We are loosed.
2. तूं सोडिला जानोस m. -ली जानोस f. -लें जानेंस n. Thou art loosed.	2. तुम्ही सोडिले जाना m. -ल्या जाना f. -लीं जाना n. You are loosed.
3. ने सोडिला जानो m. -ली जानी f. -लें जानें n. He, she, or it is loosed.	3. ते सोडिले जानात m. ल्या-ल्या जानात f. तीं -लीं जानात n. They are loosed.

The rest of the tenses may be formed in the above manner.

CHAPTER XIII.

PARTICLES OR INDECLINABLE WORDS.

I. THE ADVERB.

(क्रियाविशेषण अव्यय.)

156. An Adverb is a word which is used to qualify any attribute as तो फार शहाणा आहे He is very wise ; निकडे जा Go there.

157. Adverbs may be divided into the following classes :—

(1) ADVERBS OF TIME ; कालवाचक क्रियाविशेषण.

a. Point of time ; तेव्हां then, आतां, एव्हां now, केव्हां when, पूर्वीं before, सांप्रत at present, नंतर afterwards, तूर्त presently, लवकर soon, आज to-day, उद्यां to-morrow, काल yesterday, परवां two days ago, or two days hence, तेव्हां then, अगोदर formerly, मग hereafter, झटकन् instantly, अकस्मात्, एकाएकीं suddenly, नुक्तें lately, एकदम at once, तात्काळ immediately.

b. Duration of time ; नेहमीं always, सतत continually, लवकर quickly, नित्य daily, कधीं ever, कधीं नाहीं never, दिवसानुदिवस or दिवसेंदिवस day after day, प्रतिदिवसीं, रोजचा रोज, and रोजरोज daily.

Note. दिवसानुदिवस &c. express an act that daily increases or decreases, while प्रतिदिवश &c. do not involve any notion of an increase or diminution.

(2) ADVERBS OF PLACE ; स्थलवाचक क्रियाविशेषण.

c. Rest in a place; तेथें there, येथें here, जेथें तेथें everywhere, कोठें नाहीं nowhere, वर above, खालीं below, मध्यें within, मागें behind, पुढें before, पल्याड beyond, कोठें where ?

d. Motion to or from a place; इकडे hither, तिकडे thither, इकडून hence, तिकडून thence, सभोंवतें around, समीप, जवळ near, दूर far, पलिकडे beyond.

(3) Adverbs of Manner; प्रकारदर्शक क्रियाविशेषण.

e. Manner; भसें so, येणेंप्रमाणें thus, बरें well, शहाणपणानें wisely. (See Adverbs in नें under Derivation), एन्हवीं, उगाच, उगीच, उगेंच, उगा merely, or for no reason.

f. Degree; फार very, अगदीं quite, जरा nearly, a little, किंचित् scarcely, मात्र only, अधिक more, कमी less, अतिशय exceedingly, अत्यंत eminently; हळू slowly.

Note. च, ही, ना, पण, are emphatic adverbs; *e.g.,* तूंच ये You alone come; तूंही ये You too come; तूं ना येतोस Are you coming or is somebody else coming? तूं पण ये You too come.

(4) Adverbs of Quantity; परिमाणवाचक क्रियाविशेषण अव्यय.

g. Measure; फार much, थोडा little, पुरें enough, कांहीं or -सा somewhat, अगदीं entirely, बहुत much.

h. Number or Order; एकदां once, शंभरपट or शंभरशा a hundred-fold, पहिल्यानें, प्रथमतः firstly, दुसऱ्यानें secondly, शेवटीं, अखेरीं lastly.

(5) Adverbs of Mood; स्वीकारार्थक or अनुमोदनार्थक.

(i) Affirmation; होय yes, खचीत certainly, निःसंशय undoubtedly, खरोखर truly.

(j) Negation; नाहीं, न, ना not, किमपि नाहीं, विलकूल नाहीं not at all कधीं नाहीं never.

(k) Probability and Doubt; कदाचित् perhaps, बहुधा for the most part.

(6) Adverbs of Relation; संबंधवाचकें :—

जेव्हां when, जेथें तेथें wherever, जेथें कोठें wheresoever.

(7) Adverbs of Interrogation; प्रश्नार्थक :—

केव्हां when? कोठें where? कशाला why? कोणीकडे where? कां why?

(8) Adverbs of Imitation; अनुकरणवाचक :—

झणझणां, फटकन, गटागट, &c.

II. THE PREPOSITION.

(शब्दयोगी अव्यय.)

158. A Preposition is a word which shows the relation of a noun or pronoun to some other word in the sentence; तो जाग्यावर बसला He took his seat.

159. Prepositions relate nouns or pronouns to other nouns or pronouns, or to verbs or adjectives. They express the following relations :—

(*a*) *Time and space;* आंत, ठायीं, मध्यें in, वर on, समीप, सन्निध, पासीं near, बाहेर out, खालीं under, मागें behind, formerly, पुढें before, in future, आलिकडे on this side, पलिकडे on that side, नंतर after, पूर्वीं before (in time), समोर before (in place).

(*b*) *Motion to or from;* कडे at, पासून from, prepositions in ऊन, as वरून from above, खालून from below, पर्यंत, पावेतों till.

(*c*) *Instrumentality;* कडून, करवीं, हातीं, द्वारें, or रा by, or through.

(*d*) *Miscellaneous Relations;* शिवाय, वांचून, विना without, विषयीं about, बदल instead of, खेरीज besides, पुरता enough, पैकीं, साठीं for, सवें, सहीत, सहवर्तमान with.

160. *Observations on Prepositions.*

(1) The prepositions generally inflect the word after which they are placed; as घरावर on the house. Sometimes they do not inflect the word; as सकाळपर्यंत till the morning.

(2) The prepositions are, sometimes, joined to the genitive of nouns; as घरा या बाहेर or घराबाहेर out of the house.

(3) Prepositions ending in आ are, sometimes, inflected to agree in gender and number, in order to agree with the nouns to which they refer; as त्या समोवते or -नाले वीस हत्ती उभे होते Twenty elephants stood around him.

Note. The noun with which a preposition agrees is the subject or the object of the sentence in which the preposition, together with the noun which it governs, stands as a prepositional or adverbial phrase; घराभोंवतालें पाणीं शिंप Sprinkle water round the house; ती त्या सभोंवतालीं नाचली She danced round it.

(4) When a prepositional phrase or a simple preposition is used as an attributive, it takes an adjective suffix; त्यांविषयींची गोष्ट The story respecting them; पुण्यासभोंवतील गांव The villages round about Poona; नद्रोपलिकडलें तळें The tank beyond the river; पलिकडला गांव Yonder village.

(5) Some prepositions are used both before and after nouns; as तूं विनघोर बैस Be without fear; मी रुपये घेतल्याविना जाणार नाहीं I will not go unless I take the rupees.

161. III. THE CONJUNCTION.

A Conjunction is a word used to connect the different parts of an extended sentence or two affirmations.

Note. 1. Even when the conjunction appears only to connect two words, it really connects two sentences.

2. Prepositions relate two notions; conjunctions two sentences.

162. The conjunctions are thus classified:—

(1) Conjunctions which join sentences together, as well as unite their meaning, and which are called *Copulative Conjunctions*; आणि and, अणखी and, म्हणजे that is, व and, कीं that.

(2) Conjunctions which join two sentences together, but disconnect their meaning, and which are called *Disjunctive Conjunctions*; किंवा, अथवा, कीं or, नाहींतर nevertheless, किंबहुना nay, तथापि notwithstanding, पण, परंतु but.

IV. THE INTERJECTION.

(केवलप्रयोगी अव्यय.)

163. An Interjection is a word which expresses any sudden wish or emotion of the mind, but no definite thought.

Interjections may express—

(1) *Sudden joy* हर्षबोधक; ओहो, हीयो.

(2) *Sudden approbation* धन्यताबोधक; वाहवा, ठीक, भलेशाबास.

(3) *Sudden surprise* आश्चर्यबोधक; आहा, व:, वाहवा, भयय, अलल, अहाहा.

(4) *Sudden displeasure* धिक्कारबोधक; (*a*) *contempt*, छे, छन्, छो, छिछो, धिक्, फें; (*b*) *disgust*, इइञ, इहयो, इहर्यो, शिव; (*c*) *reproach*, हत्त, उदर; (*d*) *prohibition*, ऊंहूं or ऊंहूं; (*e*) *indifference*, अं.

CHAPTER X.

DERIVATIONS.

164. Words are traceable to roots.

165. A root is that part of a word which cannot be reduced to a simpler or more original form, either in that language, or family of languages to which it belongs.

166. Maráṭhí is derived from two distinct stocks of languages, the Turanian and the Aryan.

167. The Turanian languages are the Turkish, Chinese, Canarese, Telegu, Tamil, Malyallam, &c., and the Aryan are the Greek, Latin, Teutonic, Gothic, Slavonic, Zend, Sanskṛit, and their several dialects.

168. The Turanian is the oldest element in Maráṭhí, and is perceptible in the vocables of general use among the lower classes, and in the business of ordinary life. The imitative particles, and the words beginning with the cerebrals and the letter झ, are chiefly of Turanian origin.

169. Maráṭhí, as we now find it, appears to be chiefly derived from Sanskṛit, to which it is indebted for nearly nine-tenths of its vocables. The Sanskṛit words exist in it either in their native or modified form; and the changes of the modified forms are traceable to the various dialects and languages, through which they have come into it.

170. The Sanskrit dialects, from which Maráthí and the other modern Aryan languages of India, such as the Hindusthání, Gujaráti, Bengálí, &c., are derived, were called Prákṛit or vulgar tongues, by way of distinction from the parent language, whose name etymologically signifies "a polished tongue" (सं well, कृत made = संस्कृत).

171. Maráthí bears the closest affinity to Mágdhí, a Prákṛit dialect which flourished in Mágdha or Bahár, and which was probably first introduced into Maháráshṭra by the Buddhist missionaries in 264 A.D.

172. The following are the principal changes which Sanskrit words have undergone in the Prákṛit dialects:—

(1) The long vowels have been contracted into short vowels; as मार्गः a way = मग्गो; दीपः long दिग्यो.

(2) The double letters formed by the consonants of different organs have been changed to consonants of the same organs; as ईश्वरः God = ईस्सरो; दीर्घः long = दिग्घो; or one of the letters is dropt; as दर्शनं sight, दसणं.

(3) The similar and dissimilar vowels have been substituted for each other; as सिंदुरं red lead = सेंदुरं; देवरः a brother-in-law = दिभरो.

(4) The vowels ऋ, ॠ and ऌ have been changed to रि or री, इ or ई, and लि or ली, लु; as ऋणं a debt = रिणं; भृंगः a beetle = भिंगो.

(5) The aspirates and ह are interchangeable; as मुखं a mouth = मुहं; गुह्यं a secret = गुझं.

(6) The Visarga has been changed to ओ; as मेघः a cloud = मेहो; केशः a hair = केसो.

(7) The dentals have been displaced by the cerebrals; as ऐरावतः an elephant = ऐरावणो; दंशः a sting = डंसो.

(8) The unaspirates are sometimes changed to aspirates; as पनसः = फणसो.

173. The Prákrit words underwent a change before they assumed their present Maráthí forms. The following are the three principal changes :—

I. The compound letters have been displaced by simple letters : as घम्मो (धर्मः S.) perspiration = घाम; गब्भो (गर्भः S.) = गाभा pith; जग्गो (योग्यः S.) = जोगा fit.

II. The initial short vowel, followed by a double letter, has been lengthened, when the double letter has been changed to a simple letter; as निद्दा (निद्रा S.) = नीज sleep; दुद्धं (दुग्धं S.) = दूध milk; पवखो (पक्षः S.) = पाख a wing.

III. The final ओ, substituted for the Sanskrit Visarga, is dropt or changed to आ; as घंटो (घटः S.) = घाट a bell; करंडो (करंडः S.) = करंडा a basket; ओट्ठो (ओष्ठः S.) = ओंठ a lip; जग्गो (योग्यः S.) = जोगा fit.

Note. In some Maráthí words the ओ still retains its place; as जो who = यः S. तो he = सः S.

174. The Maráthí language, thus derived, has become the vernacular of ten millions of souls; it combines the dignity and vigour of the Sanskrit with the softness and pliancy of the Prákrit. Its vocabulary has received valuable contributions from the Arabic, Persian, Hindusthání; Gujarátí, and several European languages, so that it is the most copious, the most learned, and the most polished of the modern Indian languages. It has been, since the rise of the Maráthá power, the language of several Native courts, and possesses some literature, both in prose and verse, of comparatively great merit.

Maráthí words have in their turn become the sources of new words, and claim the rank of roots. They have been designated in this book *Marāṭhí Roots*. We give below two illustrations.

Root: बोलणें to speak (ब्रू S. to speak).

Nouns: बोल word; बोलणें speaking; बोलवा, बोलवाय, popular talk; बोलचाली conversation; बोलावणें invitation; बोली a language; अबोला reserve.

Adjectives: बोलका eloquent, बोलगडा loquacious; बोलता that speaks.

Verbs: बोलणें to speak; बोलाविणें to call.

Root: बांधणें to build (बंध् S. to bind).

Nouns: बांध an embankment; बांधण damming up; बांधणावळ the cost of building; बांधणी the style of building; बांधणें the rubbish used for damming; बांधण fixing material; बांधा structure; बांधणी a passage through a field; बांधारा the raised boundary of a field; बांधावळ structure; बांधील binding of rice into bundles; बांधें or बांधाळें a parasitical plant; बांधेकरी a villager without landed property; बांधोळी a small embankment; बांदरी the horizon.

Adjectives: बांधणी relating to a ground; बांधील bound by favours; बांधोव built.

Verbs: बांधटणें To be so advanced as to have its stone fully formed, a mango; बांधणें to bind; बांधाटणें, see बांधटणें.

175. Words are derived from Marāṭhí roots in six ways. They are these :—

(1) By modifying the vowels and consonants of which the simple word is composed; as बांध a dam, बांधा a shape, from बांधणें to bind; डोळू an eyelet, or a little hole—from डोळा an eye; पाडणें to fell, from पडणें to fall.

(2) By joining letters or particles before and after a word, *i. e.*, by means of *prefixes* and *affixes*; अ + तूट = अतूट unbroken; राग + ईट = रागीट passionate.

(3) By the union of the above two methods; as उल्लूक the head of a fish, from डोळा an eye.

(4) By doubling the simple word; दाणेदुणें grain, &c., from दाणे grain.

(5) By two or more words joined to express one notion, and both the words retaining a place in the formation; as काळमांजर a polecat, from काळें black, and मांजर a cat.

(6) By uniting two words so that one of the words is lost; तेलवणीं = तेल + पाणीं water and oil; आंबसाण = आंबट sour + घाण smell.

176. The first class of words are called *Primary Derivatives*; the second two classes of words, *Secondary Derivatives*; the fourth class, *Reduplicatives*; and the last two, *Compounds*.

I. Primary Derivatives.

177. The Maráthí roots are comparatively few, and numerous words are derived from them by modifying their form. We can notice here only the Potentials and the Causals.

178. I. *The Potentials*. These verbs are derived by inserting व between the gerundial termination and the verbal root; as करणें to do, करवणें to be able to do. (Sec. 126.)

179. II. *The Causals*. These verbs are formed by inserting विज between the root and the gerundial termination; as करणें to do, करविणें to cause to do; देणें to give, देवविणें to cause to give.

Note. The form करविणें is preferable to करवणें and करिवणें.

The causal suffix वि or व is the corruption of the Sanskrit particle य or भय, used in forming causals; as करोति he does, कारयति he causes to do. The य is changed to ए or आवें, य and व being interchangeable letters.

When वि is affixed to transitive verbs, they become causals, denoting the instrumental agency of a person distinct from the subject of the verb; but when वि is affixed to intransitive verbs, they become transitive, and not causative; निजणें to sleep, निजविणें to cause to sleep, निजविविणें to cause to make to sleep.

Some intransitive verbs modify the final vowel of the root before the suffix वि; as फितणें to be taken in, फिताविणें or फितविणें to seduce; बोलणें to speak, बोलाविणें or बोलविणें to call.

When verbs are derived from nouns or adjectives by the suffix आव, those in simple आव are intransitive, and in आवि are transitive; as आंबट sour, आंबटावणें to be turned sour, आंबटाविणें to make sour; दुःख pain, दुःखावणें to be hurt, दुःखविणें to hurt.

180. Some intransitive verbs do not take the participle वि to form the intransitives, but simply change the initial vowel of the root. In this particular they resemble the Sanskrit causal verbs, which lengthen the initial vowel of the root; as खनति he digs, खानयति he causes to dig.

1. The intransitives that lengthen the initial अ :—

    चरणें to graze, चारणें to feed.

    टळणें to pass by, टाळणें to remove.

    तरणें to float or to be saved, तारणें to save.

    दबणें to be crushed, दाबणें to crush.

    पडणें to fall, पाडणें to fell.

    मरणें to die, मारणें to kill.

    सरणें to move on (v. i.), सारणें to move on (v. t.)

(2) The intransitives that undergo both a vowel and a consonantal change :—

    फिटणें to get loose, फेडणें to loose.

    तुटणें to break, तोडणें to break.

    सुटणें to get loose, सोडणें to loose.

(3) Some intransitives modify only the consonant; as फाटणें to tear (*v. i.*), फाडणें to tear (*v. t.*).

181. The causals of these transitive verbs are formed by affixing वि; as सुटणें to get loose, सोडणें to loose, and सोडविणें to cause to loose.

II. Secondary Derivatives.

PREFIXES.

182. The particles called prefixes (उपसर्ग) and suffixes (प्रत्यय) used in Maráṭhí are derived chiefly from the Sanskṛit. The Sanskṛit grammarians mention in all twenty particles (अव्यय), which are as follows:—

अति beyond; अतिक्रम passing beyond; अतिस्नेह, अतिशहाणा.

अधि over; अधिदेव a superior god; अधिकार authority.

अनु after; अनुसरण going after; अनुज born after; अनुनासिक.

अप off; अपांक्त away from caste; अपहरण.

अपि upon; अपिभान a placing upon, a covering.

अभि towards; अभिमुख having the face towards.

अव down; अवतार the crossing down, an incarnation.

आ near to; आकार form; आग्रह entreaty.

उद् up; उत्साह ardour.

उप next, below; उपसर्ग a prefix; उपकार.

दुर्, दुस् bad; दुर्गुण a bad quality; दुराचार; दुर्बुद्धि.

नि into, downwards; निर्वाह conducting; निःपतन fallen down.

निः, निर without; निर्दोषि without blemish.

परा back, away; पराङ्मुख having the face turned back; पराजय defeat.

परि around; पर्यटन to walk round about.

प्र before; प्रभु the being before, a lord; प्रधान.

प्रति back; प्रतिबिंब a reflected beam; प्रत्युत्तर.

वि apart; वियोग disjoining, a separation; विधवा.

सम् together with; संगम going with, a junction; संबंध.

सु well; सुरूप good-looking, सुविचार.

183. Besides these, the following prefixes are of general use in the Maráthí language :—

अ, अन्, not; अपार boundless; अबोला reserve; अचूक.

कम (H.) deficient; कमजोर weak.

कु bad; कुकर्म a bad deed; कुविचार, कुपात्र, कुरंग.

गैर (A.) other; गैरसमज a misunderstanding; गैरखर्च.

दर, हर (H.) each; दरमहा every month; दरदिवस.

न not; नास्तिक an atheist.

ना (H.) not; नापसंद disapproved; नामर्द.

पर another; परजन a stranger; परदेसी, परगांव.

पुनर् again; पुनर्जन्म, regeneration; पुनर्विवाह.

पेश (P.) before; पेशवा a leader.

बद (P.) bad; बदकाम a bad deed; बदनाम.

बिन (H.) without; बिनचूक without a mistake; बिनहरकत.

बे (P.) without; बेइलाज without remedy; बेडोल, बेशरम.

सत् good; सत्कर्म a good work; सज्जन.

सर (H.) head; सर सुभेदार the head subhedár.

सह with, together with; सहवास intercourse; संदोष.

स्व one's own; स्वदेश a native country; स्वबुद्धि.

SUFFIXES.

184. There are numerous suffixes in the Maráthí language, which it is impossible to enumerate in this small work. The following are, however, the most useful of them :—

I. Nouns.

I. *Abstract Nouns.*

Pure Maráthí abstract nouns are derived from adjectives by affixing पण n. and पणा m. to adjectives; वाईट bad, वाईटपण or पणा badness.

These affixes do not differ from each other in anything else but in the gender. When they are joined to adjectives ending in आ m., the final vowel is changed to ए; भला honest, भलेपण or पणा honesty. चांगला is changed either to चांगले or चांगूल before the suffixes.

Words of Sanskrit origin take the suffixes ता f., त्व n., and य n. to form abstract nouns, and these particles are affixed to substantives as well as adjectives.

Note. When य is affixed, the initial vowel is changed into a corresponding long (वृद्धि) vowel.

Examples.

गुरु (adj.) heavy; गुरुता, गुरुत्व, गौरव heaviness.
लघु (adj.) light; लघुता, लघुत्व, लाघव lightness.
दृढ (adj.) hard; दृढता, दृढत्व, दार्ढ्य hardness.
मित्र (sub.) a friend; मित्रता, मित्रत्व, मैत्र friendship.
ब्राह्मण (sub.) a Bráhman; ब्राह्मणता, ब्राह्मणत्व, ब्राह्मण्य.

Note. Some Sanskrit words do not take all the three suffixes; as मुनि a sage, मौन्य or मौन reserve.

Note. Some words simply lengthen the initial vowel; as कुमार a youth, कौमार.

Words of Hindusthání origin take the following suffixes :—

इ or आई; भला honest, भलाई honesty; भीट, भिटाई obstinacy :—आ or आई; गरम warm, गरमा or गरमाई warmth :—आस ; मिठें sweet, मिठास sweetness :— ती ; कम little, कमती deficiency.

2. *Nouns of Agency*:—

M. आड्या; वाट a way, वाटाड्या a guide.
M. आरी; पूजा worship, पुजारी a worshipper.
S. ई; पाप sin, पापी a sinner.
M. कर; गाव a village, गावकर a villager.
S. कार; रत्न a jewel, रत्नकार a jeweller.
H. गर; जीन a saddle, जिनगर a saddler.
H. गार; शिकल, शिकलगार a cutler.
M. स्थ; कोंकण Konkaṇ, कोंकणस्थ a Konkaṇí.
H. दार; सुभा, सुभेदार a subhedár.
H. बंद; नाल a horse-shoe, नालबंद a farrier.
M. वान; गाडी a carriage, गाडीवान coachman.
H. वाला; दूध milk, दूधवाला a milkman.

3. *Nouns denoting office, condition, &c.*:—

ई; सराफ, सराफी money-changing.
की; पाटील, पाटिलकी a pátílship.
गिरी; गुलाम, गुलामगिरी slavery.
ड़ाई; सोदा, सोदेड़ाई blackguardism.

4. *Diminutive Nouns*:—

ई; गोळा a ball, गोळी a shot.
डी; पलंग a bedstead, पलंगडी a small bedstead.
रूं; वाघ a tiger, वाघरूं the cub of a tiger.

II. ADJECTIVES.

1. *Adjectives denoting of or pertaining to*:—

ई; कोंकण (n.), कोंकणी belonging to the Konkaṇ.
ईल; आत (prep.), आतील internal.
चा, ची, चें; घर (n.), घरचा -ची -चें household.
ला, ली, लें; तेयें (adv.), तेयला -ली -लें belonging to that place.
वट; रान (n.), रानवट belonging to a desert.

2. *Denoting made or acted upon :—*

इव; बांध (v.), बांधीव built.

पट or वट; धू (v.), धुपट or धुवट washed.

3. *Denoting full of or abounding :—*

आडू; खेळ (n.), खेळाडू frolicsome.
आळू; झोंप (n.), झोंपाळू sleepy.
कट; मळ (n.), मळकट filthy.
कर; खोडी (n.), खोडकर mischievous.
खोर; कज्जा (n.), कज्जेखोर quarrelsome.
ईट; राग (n.), रागीट angry.
इत; आनंद (n.), आनंदित joyful.
मंत; बुद्धि (n.), बुद्धिमंत wise.
वंत; धन (n.), धनवंत rich.
इष्ट; कोप (n.), कोपिष्ट angry.
ई; लोभ (n.), लोभी covetous.
मान्; बुद्धि (n.), बुद्धिमान् intelligent.
वान्; धन (n.), धनवान् rich.
रूप; दुःख (n.), दुःखरूप painful.

4. *Denoting likeness or manner :—*

कट; पोर (n.), पोरकट childish.
चट; पाणी (n.), पाणचट waterish.
या; बायको (n.), बायक्या womanish.

5. *Denoting diminution :—*

ट; उंच (adj.), उंचट highish.
सर; काळा (adj.), काळसर blackish.
सा; लहान (adj.), लहानसा -सी -सें littleish.

6. *Denoting doing* :—

का; मार (n.), मारका Given to beating.
रा; खाजणें (v.), खाजरा Itch-producing.
खाऊ; भाउ (n), भाउखाऊ A bawd.
भरू; पोट (n.), पोटभरू Filling the stomach.

III. VERBS.

Verbs are derived from other words by the use of the suffix णें, the gerundial termination. They are chiefly derived from nouns and adjectives; thus,—

दुःख (n.), दुःखणें To pain.
झपाटा (n.), झपाटणें To despatch (a business).
इच्छा (n.), इच्छिणें To wish.
मळकट (adj.), मळकटणें To be defiled.
आंबट (adj.), आंबटावणें To turn sour.
नागवा (adj.), नागविणें To strip naked.
रोड (adj.), रोडणें To become thin.

Note. The causals, and the potentials, derived from verbs, have been noticed under the Primary Derivatives.

III. Reduplicatives.

186. The Reduplicatives are formed by doubling the original word; भाकरी-भिकरी.

187. They are formed in four ways, viz.—1st, By simply doubling the original word; 2ndly, By repeating the general sense and sound of the original word; 3rdly, By repeating only the sense of the original word; 4thly, By repeating only the sound of the original word. Of these formations, those of the 1st class only can be distinguished from compounds.

188. The true reduplicatives are such words as भाकरीभिकरी, धोंडागिडा, खडेउडे, धोंउधोंपट, दाणेदुणे, &c., of which only one part has a distinct sense. The English equivalents are chit-chat, tittle-tattle, slip-slop, hurly-burly, &c.

189. Sometimes the original word, which is a verb, is doubled, and the first part of it adds आ to the final letter, to signify *hurried* or *active doing*; as बांधबांध, साधासाध, तोडातोड, &c. The whole word may take ई at the end of it; as बांधबांधी, साधासाधी, &c.

190. The reduplicatives are chiefly derived from what are called अनुकरण शब्द or imitative particles, which are formed in imitation of the sounds they represent; thus चटचट is in imitation of the sound of *lashing* or *caning*, the equivalents of which in English are "smack," " bang," &c.

In forming these reduplicatives, either the original particle is repeated, or another of similar sound is joined; as सटसट or सटकण; झटझट or झटकन -कर -पट -दिनी -दिशीं, &c.

191. There are numberless imitative particles in use in Maráṭhí, and every day new ones come into existence. They have become the source of many useful words of constant occurrence in the discourse of the learned and the illiterate. They are, by their origin, adverbs, expressing the *manner* of an action, but are used as nouns, adjectives, &c. Thus बुळबुळ is an adverb, an imitative of light showering, from which the following classes of words are derived :—

Nouns :—

1. बुळबुळी A particular plant.
2. बुळबुळीत ⎫
3. बुळबुळाट ⎬ Greasiness.
4. बुळबुळण ⎭
5. बुळका A porpoise.
6. बुळकी, बुळकांडी A loose stool.

Adjectives :—

1. बुळबुळीत Greasy.
2. बुळा Impotent.
3. बुळकट Slippery from grease.
4. बुळका Slack.

Note. The reduplicated nouns are used with particular verbs; as बुळबुळ लाव -माड -वहा -लाग -सूट -चाल -हो.

Note. When the suffix आट is applied to them, they denote that the action which they express is wrought to excess; as थरथराट excessive trembling.

Note. The imitative adverbs express greater force when their final vowels are modified; as झडाझड or झडझडां is more emphatic than झडझड : चटाचट or चटचटां than चटचट.

IV. Compounds.

192. A compound is a union of two or more words, expressing one idea; as रण + भूमि = रणभूमि a battle-field.

193. The elements that enter into composition do, or do not, retain a place in the compound. Sometimes two or more words express one simple notion without *formally* entering into composition. Hence there are three general classes of compounds, viz., the *True*, the *Obscure*, and the *Apparent*. Thus :—

1. *True Compounds;* पोळी + पाट = पोळपाट a table for rolling out cakes.

2. *Obscure Compounds:* करपट + घाण = करपटाण the smell of singed food.

3. *Apparent Compounds;* हाताचा कुशळ expert.

Note. None but words of cognate origin should be combined; there are, however, some exceptions in Maráthí of long-established usage. Thus,

वस्त्रगाळ Strained through a cloth = वस्त्र S. + गाळ M.
गायमुख A cow's mouth = गाय M. + मुख S.
खरेदीपत्र A bond = खरेदी H. + पत्र S.
ज्यडज्य कचेरी A Judge's office = ज्यडज्य Eng. + कचेरी H.

I. TRUE COMPOUNDS.

194. In Maráthí only two words are generally combined, and the compounds thus formed are either substantives, adjectives, or adverbs.

I. The Substantive Compound is used as a substantive, and its first word determines or describes the other, or the two words together denote a collective notion.

When the first word describes the second, it is either an adjective, or a noun used attributively; when both the words hold a similar position in the compound, they bear to each other a co-ordinate relation. These two classes of compounds are designated *Determinative* and *Copulative* respectively.

II. When a substantive compound is used attributively, it is called an Adjective Compound.

III. When two or more words are so combined that the compound indicates an adverbial relation, it is called an Adverbial Compound.

195. I. SUBSTANTIVE COMPOUNDS.

I. *The Determinative Compounds.*

1. In the determinative compounds are included the compounds that are designated तत्पुरुष, कर्मधारय, and द्विगु by the Sanskrit grammarians. In the *Tatpurush*, the first word indicates a case-relation, and the second word governs it in that case; thus, गजमोजणी Measuring by rule = गजानें + मोजणी. In the *Karmadháraya*, the first word is an adjective, or a noun used adjectively; as तांबडमाती Red earth = तांबडी + माती; विद्याधन Treasure of knowledge—*literally*, Knowledge which is like a treasure = विद्या + धन. In the *Dvigu* the first is a numeral adjective, and the second is the noun which it qualifies; पंच-पाळें A kind of cruet consisting of five vessels.

Note. The first word drops its inflections; thus in गजमोजणी, the case-ending नें is dropt, and in तांबडमाती, the feminine inflection ई is dropt.

Note. The *Tatpurush* compound is *Karmadháraya*, when the first word is not supposed to express a case-relation.

Note. When the first word in the *Karmadháraya* compound is a noun, it implies often likeness or analogy; as विद्याधन Knowledge which is like a treasure.

Note. In the Sanskṛit compounds introduced into Maráthí, sometimes the first word of the *Tatpurush* or the *Karmadháraya* comes last; thus, in राजहंस King of the geese, which is a *Tatpurush* compound, the governing word comes first; so also नरसिंव्ह A man like a lion, which is a *Karmadháraya* compound, the qualifying word comes last.

Note. Words, taking a deprivative particle before them, as अब्राम्हण A non-Bráhman, &c., are called नञ्तत्पुरुष.

Note. The English equivalents to the above three kinds of determinative compounds are as follows:—

1. *The Tatpurush*: Time-keeper, steam-boat, sea-breeze, tea-spoon, &c.
2. *The Karmadháraya*: A blackbird, mankind.
3. *The Dvigu*: A twelvemonth.

Not. In the *Tatpurush* compound, the first word may be any other than the nominative case; thus—

1st. *The Accusative Tatpurush*: लाचखाऊ A bribe-receiver; ग्रंथकर्ता An author. It indicates the thing which a person does.

2nd. *The Instrumental Tat.*: हातचरक A mill turned by the hand; ईश्वरदत्त Given by God; मनःकल्पित Invented by the mind. It indicates the instrument by which a thing is done.

3rd. *The Dative Tat.*: बाजारवाडा The market-house; रणखांब A war-post; विद्यागृह A school; शरणागत Come for protection. It indicates the purpose for which a thing is designed or done.

4th. *The Ablative Tat.*: चोरभय Fear arising from thieves; रोगदुःख Pain arising from sickness; जातिभ्रष्ट Fallen from caste. It indicates the source from which a thing originates.

5th. *The Genitive Tat.*: घरधनी A householder; विद्याभ्यास The study of science. It indicates the relation of origin or possession.

6th. *The Locative Tat.*: धुळाक्षरें Letters in sand; पाणकोंबडा A water-fowl; अंडज Produced in an egg. It indicates the thing in which anything is, or is done.

2. *Copulative Compounds.*

196. In the copulative compounds two or more words are combined which would otherwise be connected by the copulative conjunction "and;" as शेलापागोटें shawl and turban. The English equivalents are "bread and butter," "rice and curry," &c.

These compounds are designated द्वंद्व by the Sanskrit grammarians.

Note. This compound has generally the same number and gender as its last member; as नाकडोळे Nose and eyes (plu. m.), घरदार (sing. n.).

Note. But when the names of animate and rational beings form both the members, the compound is either singular or plural, according to the sense it may convey. It is plural if it specifies *all the objects comprehensively*, but singular if it specifies *an individual by his general character*; तेथें कुणबीमाळी जमले होते All belonging to the various tribes or grades of peasants had assembled there (plu.); कोण कुणबी माळी आला होता Some one of the tribes or grades of peasants had come; नवरा- नवरी husband and wife (f. sing.), आईबाप (m. plu.)

Note. Some copulative compounds inflect the last member, and assume the neuter plural ending एं; as आईबाप or आईबापें Father and mother; स्त्रीपुरुषें Man and wife; मायलेकरें Mother and child.

197. There are what are called Reduplicative copulative compounds in Maráṭhí, and they are divided into the following classes:—

1. Those formed by *repeating the general sense and sound* of the original words; अंधळापांगळा Blind and lame; झाडझूड, लंगडालुळा, सगासोयरा, वेणीफणी, अर्थऋणापांघरूण, &c. The English equivalents are "wear and tear," "rattle and clatter," "worn and torn," &c.

2. Those formed by *repeating the general sense alone* of the original word; आणभाप, काजळकुंकूं, लांकूडफांटें, श्वेतमळा, भातभाजी, जोखमाप, &c. The English equivalents are "thorn and thistle," "pride and passion," "patch and piece," "sorrowing and suffering," &c.

3. Those formed by *repeating the general sound alone* of the original word; as डोचकें कीं बोंचकें The head or the bundle, डोकें कीं फोकें, &c. The English equivalents are "by hook or by crook," &c.

Note. These formations indicate the hurried or rash settlement of an affair. Some other equivalents are संक्षमोक्ष, द्याहानद्दी, &c.

4. Those formed by combining words of opposite signification, but derived from the same root; as धर्माधर्म = धर्म + अधर्म right and wrong, कार्याकार्य &c. The English equivalents are "right and wrong," "young and old," "white and black," &c.

II. Adjective Compounds.

198. When a *whole compound* is used attributively, it is called an adjective compound (बहुव्रीहि). Thus, घोडमुख the face of a horse (a substantive compound) denotes, also, *having the face of a horse*; thus, किन्नर सर्व घोडमुख होते All the Kinnars had the faces of horses.

Note. The attributive compound stands sometimes for the object which it describes, and suggests it: then it is a substantive: thus, गजानन is either "having the head of an elephant" (an adjective Bahuvrîhi), or "one who has the head of an elephant," (a substantive Bahuvrîhi), and since in the Hindû mind a human being with the head of an elephant is associated with Ganpati, the compound गजानन suggests the god Ganpati. लंबकर्ण signifies *having long ears*, or the *long-eared*, and since an ass has long ears, लंबकर्ण "or the long-eared" suggests *an ass*. The English equivalents are "left-handed," "high-minded," &c.

199. Any one of the compounds specified under the substantive compounds can become an adjective. Thus—

1. { *Tatpurush* } सभाधैर्य Boldness in an assembly.
   { *Adj.* } सभाधैर्याचा Having boldness in an assembly.

2. { *Karmadháraya* } कृष्णवर्ण A black colour.
   { *Adj.* } कृष्णवर्णी Having a black colour.

3. { *Dvigu* } चतुर्मुख Four faces.
   { *Adj.* } चतुर्मुखी Having four faces.

4. { *Dwandwa* } कुणबीमाळी A farmer and gardener.
   { *Adj.* } कुणब्यामाळ्याचा Of a farmer and gardener.

III. Adverbial Compounds.

200. In the adverbial compounds the first word is an adverb, and the whole is used adverbially; as दरदिवस every day.

201. The following are a few examples to illustrate the elements that enter into composition in the adverbial compounds:—

1. *A particle and a noun;* दरदिवस every day; यथाक्रम regularly.

2. *Two particles;* जेथेंकोठें anywhere; यथातथा so and so.

3. *A particle and an adjective;* यथायोग्य suitably; यथातृप्त to the fill.

4. *A particle and a participle;* यथायुक्त rightly.

5. *A particle and an inflected noun;* as आजइवशीं to-day; हरवेळीं every time; यथाज्ञानें according to one's knowledge.

II. Obscure Compounds.

202. There are numerous words in Maráthí in which composition is concealed by the incompleteness of one of the elements, or of both; hence they appear as derivatives, and sometimes even as primitives. Such compounds exist, also, in the English language, and they forcibly illustrate how a people of strong mental activity express their thoughts and notions with the greatest possible brevity. Formations of " learned length " and " thundering sound" are as foreign to the genius of Maráthí as they are to the genius of English, and although such combinations as " प्रतिज्ञाद्यादिवेदव्याकरणभाष्यकार,""गालवशौनककात्यायनशाकटायनादि," "वाल्मीकिव्यासशंकरश्रीहर्षकालिदासभवभूत्यादि," &c. may well suit the Sanskṛit, they mar and disfigure the simple and elegant language on which they are engrafted by their author.

203. In the obscure compounds of pure Maráthí origin, only one of the elements is lost, but in those of Sanskṛit origin both of the elements undergo a change. Thus—

I. Compounds of pure Maráthí Origin.

केकताड A kind of palm = केकत + ताड.
गटाणा Grain or food = गट + दाणा.
पायठा A step (of a ladder) = पाय + ठाय.
मुताट A urine-hole in a stable = मूत + ठाय.
धुपेल A scented oil of resin = धूप + तेल.
आंवसाण A sour smell = आंवट + घाण.
उभारे Rather high = उभा + अग्कार.

II. Compounds of Sanskrit Origin.

S. सुवर्णकार = Prák. सोण्णभारो = M. सोनार A goldsmith.
S. कुंभ + कार = Prák. कुंभभारो or कुंभारो = M. कुंभार A potter.
S. गर्भ + आगार = Prák. गब्भाभारो or गब्भारो = M. गाभार A sanctuary.

Note. Some English equivalents: daisy = day's eye; verdict = *vere dictum*; biscuit = *bis coctus*, &c., &c.

201. The following observations on the obscure compounds of pure Maráthí origin are important:—

(1) Maráthí words generally do not exceed four syllables; hence words in composition drop or elide some of their letters; आंवट + घाण = आंवटाण.

(2) When two consonants unite, one of them is dropt: केकत + ताड = केकताड; धूप + तेल = धुपेल.

(3) When similar letters end both the elements of the compound, one of them is dropt, but the uniting consonants undergo no change: पाय + ठाय = पायठा.

(4) In composition पा of पाणी is changed to व, and घ of घाण is changed to स or is simply dropt; as तेल + पाणी = तेलवणी; आंवट + घाण = आंवसाण or आंवटाण, or आंवष्टाण.

III. APPARENT COMPOUNDS.

205. Some words in the Marāṭhí language express a simple notion, without formally entering into composition; हाताखालचा as assistant; हाताचा कुशल expert; हाताचा जड close-fisted; धर्मांदारों कुत्रें a servant that drives away beggars.

Note. "Composition is a great excellence, and helps us to express our meaning with a brevity and clearness which case-endings alone would never have given."

Note. "The power of forming compounds exists in different languages in different degrees. There seems to be one word at least in Sanskrit of a hundred and fifty-two syllables. An English lady uses one of thirteen words and forty-two syllables."— *Dr. Angus.*

CHAPTER XV.

ON THE STRUCTURE OF GRAMMATICAL FORMS.

206. PRONOUNS.

I. The Personal Pronouns.

Singular.				Plural.	
1. Nom.	मी = अहम्मि Prák. अहं	S.	आम्ही;	अम्हे Prák.
Inst.	म्यां = मे	„	मया S.		„
Gen.	माझा = मज्झ-मे	„	मे, मम S.		„
2. Nom.	तूं = तुं	„	त्वं S.	तुह्मी;	तुम्हे Prák.
3. Nom.	तो = सो	„	सः S.	ते	ते S.
Inst.	त्यानें = तेण	„	तेन S.		
Gen.	त्याचा =	„	तस्य S.		

II. Reflexive Pronouns.

आपण = आप्पण Prák. आत्मन् S.
स्वतः   स्वतः S.

III. Relative Pronouns.

जो = जो Prák. यः S.

IV. Demonstrative Pronouns.

हा	= एसो Prák.	एष:	S. or अयं S.
असा	= एसो ,,	एष:	S.
एवडा	= ,,	यावत्	S.
इतका	= ,,	इयत्	S.
तेवडा	= ,,	तावत्	S.

V. Interrogative Pronouns.

काय	= को Prak.	क:	S.
कोण	= कोण्णो ,,	क: + अन्य:	S.
कितो	= ,,	कियत् S. कति S.	
केवढा	= ,,	ditto.	

VI. Indefinite Pronouns.

काहीं	=	किमपि S.

207. VERBS.

I. Substantive Verbs.

असणें	=		अस् S.
आहें	=	आह्मि Prák.	आस्मि.
होणें (3rd pers.)	= होन्ति	,,	भवन्ति.
होय	= होइज	,,	भवति.

208. ADVERBS.

Adverbs derived from Sanskrit.

जंव when	= जाव Prák.	यावत् (य:)
तेव्हां then	= तहि or ताहि Prák.	तस्मिन् or तदा (त:)
तंव then	= ताव	तावत् (त:)
उद्या to-morrow		उदयं
काल yesterday		कालं
भगोदर first		अग्र
परवां day before yesterday		परश्वस्
बहुधा after		बहु + धा in many ways.
नेहमी always		नियम
पूर्वीं formerly		पूर्वं

(126)

असें so = एसो Prák. = एषः (यः) S.
तसें so = तहा ,, = तथा (तः)
कसें how = कह or कहं ,, = कथं (कः)
जसें as = जहा ,, = यथा (यः)
व्यर्थें in vain ,, = वृथा
बरें well ,, = वरं
पालथें upside down = पल्लत्थं ,, = पर्यस्तं
बहुशः abundantly ,, = बहु + शस्

2. Adverbs derived from Maráthí.

(a) From Nouns and Adjectives.

जातीनें naturally = the instrumental case of जात a kind.
मोठ्यानें loudly = the instrumental case of मोठा great.
रात्रीचा by night = the genitive case of रात्र night.
रात्रीस by night = the dative case of रात्र night.
रात्रीं at night = the locative of रात्र night.
दिवसा in the day-time = of दिवस a day.
वर्षांवर्षें for years = the accusative of वर्ष a year reduplicated.

(b) From Verbs.

फिरून again = the pluperfect participle of फिरणें to return.
परतून ,, = ,, ,, of परतणें to return.
रडत crying = the present participle of रडणें to cry.

(c) From Adverbs.

एथून hence = एथ here and ऊन the ablative termination.
आंतून from inside = आंत inside and ऊन ,, ,,
वरतीं upstairs = वर up and तीं.
वरतून from upstairs = वरतीं + ऊन.
इकडे तिकडे here and there = इकडे here + तिकडे there (composition).
पटपट, पटपटां = the imitative particle पट reduplicated.

(d) From Different Parts of Speech Combined.

हिकडे hither = ही this (a pronoun) + कड a side, a noun.
तिकडे thither = ती that.   „   „
इतक्यांत in the mean time = इतका so much (a pronoun), + आंत in.
पाहिजे तेथें wherever = पाहिजे wanted, a verb + तेथें there.
कोठें तरी = कोठें where (an adv.) + तरी still.

(3) *Adverbs derived from Hindusthání.*

जरा a little, बेलाशक undoubtedly, हमेशा or शा always, जरूर positively सुमारें about.

209. POSTPOSITIONS.

Prepositions derived from Nouns :—

कडे at = कड a side.
मध्यें between = मध्य (S.) a centre.
मधून from inside = मध्य (S.) „
कारणें = कारण a reason.
ठायीं in = ठाय a place (स्थान S.)
प्रमाणें as = प्रमाण S. a proof.
संगांत with संग S. union.
संबंधीं relating to संबंध S. relation.
विषयीं about = विषय S. subject.
हस्तक = हस्त S. a hand.

(2) *From Adjectives :—*

सारखा Like = सारखा like (Prák. सरिसो = सदृशः S.)

(3) *From Verbs :—*

करितां = करणें to do (कृ S.)
करवीं = करणें to do.

(3) *From Verbs.*

करून = करण to do. (S.)
पावेतों = पावणें to reach (प्रापण S.)
लागीं = लागणें to touch (लग S.)
देखत or देखतां before, दिसणें to look (दृश् S.)

(4) *Hindusthání Prepositions.*

मार्फत through, बगर without, माफक like, बराबर with, बाबत relating to, शिवाय without.

210. CONJUNCTIONS.

Conjunctions derived from Sanskrit.

कदाचित् perhaps (S.)
तथापि still (S.)
अर्थात् virtually अर्थात् (S.)
परंतु but (S.)
अथवा or (S.)
व and (वा S.)
आणि and (अन्यः S.), अण्णो (Prák.)
पण but (परंतु or परं S.)
जरी although (यर्हि S.)
तरी still (तर्हि S. तहीं Prák.)

(2) *Derived from Maráthí words.*

कां कीं because, from कां why (S. कः).
कारण because, कारण cause.
म्हणून therefore, म्हण say.
म्हणजे that is, म्हण say.
जसें as, जसा as (pronoun).
तसें so, तसा such (ditto).

INTERJECTIONS.

(1) *Nouns* are used as interjections; शिवशिव; भाईबापरे; कपाळ; भोग.

(2) *Adjectives* are used : हुशार, वास्तविक.

(3) *Adverbs* are used : खरें, चुप्प.

(4) *Verbs* are used : पहा.

(5) *Sanskrit* interjections : हे, रे, अरे, हा, हाहा.

CHAPTER XVI.

INFLECTIONS (प्रत्यय).

211. Inflections are not " conventional signs or natural excrescences, but forms which were originally intended to convey a meaning. Whether we are still able to discern the original intention of every part of language is quite a different question; and it should be admitted, at once, that many grammatical forms, after they have been restored to their most primitive type, are still without an explanation. But with every year new discoveries are made, and we become more familiar every day with the secret ways of language.

" What is grammar, after all, but declension and conjugation, and originally declension could not have been anything but the composition of a noun with some other word expressive of number and case."—*Max Müller.*

I. NOUN INFLECTIONS (सुबंतिक प्रत्यय).

I. The Gender and Number Terminations.

212. The principal Maráṭhí gender-terminations are आ, ई, एं Sing.; ए, या, ईं Plu. These can be traced to Sanskrit inflectional changes.

17 *m a*

1. *Singular Terminations:—*

(1) The masculine आ is the modification of the Prákrit ओ, and the latter form still exists in some Maráthí grammatical forms, particularly in the pronouns, as जो who, तो he, &c.

Note. Gujarátí does not modify the Prákrit ओ: thus घोटः S., घोडो Prák., घोडो Guj. (घोडा a horse).

(2) The vowel ई is employed in Sanskrit to make up feminine forms of masculine nouns, and the Maráthí termination ई, indicating the feminine gender, is identical with it; as ब्राह्मण A male Bráhman; ब्राह्मणी The wife of a Bráhman. This feminine termination exists both in Gujarátí and Hindusthání.

(3) The neuter एं is the modification of the Prákrit and Sanskrit Anusvára; तांबें = copper = तंबं Prák. ताम्र S.; तळें A pond = तलाअं Prák.

Note. एं exists in the form उं in Gujarátí; as आंडें an egg इंडुं G. (अंड S.) This form occurs in some Maráthí words too; as बकरें or बकरुं a small goat; लेकरुं a child.

2. *The Plural Terminations:—*

(1) The masculine ए is identical with the vowel ए in which the Sanskrit numerals and pronouns end in the masculine plural. Thus—

Sing. एकः One; Plu. एके Some.
„ सः He; „ ते They.

(2) The feminine या is traceable to the plural termination यः of most Sanskrit nouns ending in ई; नदी a river, नद्यः rivers; धी thought, धियः thoughts. This plural termination is assumed, also, by Hindusthání nouns of the feminine gender.

Note. When feminine words in ई are monosyllabic and take the plural या, the ई is shortened, and या is placed before the word; as बी a seed, बिया seeds; this change in Maráthí words is based upon the inflectional changes of Sanskrit words; as in धी thought, धिया thoughts.

(131)

Note. The feminine ईण is the corruption of the Sanskrit आनी; as मानुल an uncle, मानुली or मानुलानी an aunt (मामी); पति lord, पत्नी wife.

(3) The neuter ई is a modification of the Sanskrit नि or आनि, which is changed to ई or आई in Prákrit; as जीं which = जाईं Prák. = यानि S.

II. The Case-terminations:—

Singular.

Nom.	देवः S.;	देवो Prák.;	देव	M.;	A God.
Acc.	देवं ,,	देवं ,,	देव	,,	A God.
Inst.	देवेन ,,	देवेन ,,	देवानें	,,	My God.
Dat.	देवाय ,,	,,	देवाला-स	,,	To God.
Abl.	देवात् ,,	देवादु-दो ,,	देवाहून	,,	From God.
Gen.	देवस्य ,,	देवस्स ,,	देवाचा	,,	Of God.
Loc.	देवे ,,	देवे-आम्मि ,,	देवीं-वां	,,	In God.
Voc.	देव ,,	देव ,,	देव or देवा	,,	O God.

Plural.

Nom.	देवाः	S.	देवा	Prák.;	देव	M.
Acc.	देवान्	,,	देवे-वा	,,	देव	,,
Inst.	देवैः	,,	देवहिं-हि	,,	देवानों-हीं	,,
Dat.	देवेभ्यः	,,		,,	देवाला-ना	,,
Abl.	देवेभ्यः	,,	देवाहिंतो-सुंतो ,,		देवाहून	,,
Gen.	देवानां	,,	देवाणं-ण	,,	देवाचा	,,
Loc.	देवेषु	,,	देवेसु-सुं	,,	देवां or वीं	,,
Voc.	देवाः	,,	देवा	,,	देवानों	,,

OBSERVATIONS.

(1) The accusative, both in the singular and plural number, drops the inflections in Maráṭhi.

(2) The instrumental नें, ए, नीं, ईं, हीं could be easily traced to the Prákrit and Sanskrit originals.

(3) The Prákrit is deficient in the dative terminations, for which it substitutes the genitive; the Maráṭhí स and ना are hence in all probability modifications of the Prákrit genitive endings रस and आणं or णं. The ला is a pure Maráṭhí particle, being a fragment of लागीं, the dative postposition, of frequent occurrence in Maráṭhí poetry.

(4) The Maráṭhí ablative termination हून or ऊन is a modification of the Prákrit हिंतो or सुंतो = हुंतो, the letters स and ह being interchangeable. By dropping the ओ of हुंतो, and substituting न for त, the termination हून would be obtained.

(5) The genitive चा is the modification of the Sanskrit स्य and the Prákrit रस.

Note. 1. The genitive चा has the force of an adjective suffix, thus घरचा is household. It is also employed to turn particles into adjectives; as परावरचें पाखरूं The bird on the top of the house.

2. The genitive case is the only case which is used, like an adjective, in the place of a substantive, and declined in all the cases that an adjective is; thus—

	Adjective.	Genitive.
Nom.	चांगला good.	माझा mine.
Inst.	चांगल्यानें	माझ्यानें by mine.
Dat.	चांगत्याला	माझ्याला to mine.

3. The etymology of the Sanskrit स्य from which चा is derived, is the corruption of the Sanskrit adjectival suffix त्य; as दक्षिणा south, दक्षिणास्य southern. "This *tya* is a demonstrative pronoun, the same as the Sanskrit *syas, tyad,* this or that." In Greek, adjectives are formed by adding *sios* to the noun, which is the same as the Sanskrit त्य or स्य. This *sios* is identical with the Greek genitive termination *Os = Sos.*

5. The locative ईं or आं is derived from the Prákrit singular locative आम्मि = म्मि = ई.

6. The vocative नो occurs in Prákrit in the form णो; as अग्गिणो (अग्यः) O fire.

II. The Verbal Inflections (तिङ् प्रत्यय.)

213. The personal terminations are fragments of the personal pronouns, and could be easily traced to them. Thus—

The Verbal Form.			The Pronoun.	
Sanskrit	asmi	I am;	aham	I, ma me.
Greek	eimi	,,	ego	I, me me.
Latin	sum	,,	ego	I, me me.
English	am	,,		I, me.
Prákrit	amhi	,,	ahammi	I,
Maráṭhí	áhen	,,	मी	I.

214. The Maráṭhí personal endings are modifications of the third personal pronoun तो. The pronoun is simply affixed to the base. Thus—

मर die + तो he = मरतो he dies.

मर die + ती she = मरती she dies.

मर die + तें it = मरतें it dies.

The pronouns undergo a slight change when they are employed to make up the other forms of the present tense. Their altered forms correspond to the Prákrit and Sanskrit tense-endings.

The personal endings of the first person, both in Prákrit and Sanskrit, contain a nasal, and this explains the Anusvára of the Maráṭhí forms तों, तों and तोंस are thus explained:—

1st Sing. ॱमि S. = मि Prák. = इं or ॱ M. (तो + ॱ = तों).

2nd ,, सि S. = सि Prák. = सीं or स M. (तो + स = तोंस).

In the plural personal endings the pronoun तो is modified in the 1st person to तों, in the 2nd person to ता, and in the 3rd person to तात. These plural forms are thus derived:—

1st मः S. = मु Prák. = ऊं or ॱ M. (तो + ॱ = तों).
2nd थ S. = ह Prák. = आ M. (तो + आ = ता).
3rd अन्ति S. = अनि Prák. = आत M. (तो + आत = तात).

215. In the past forms the personal endings of the present tense are combined with the ल of the past participle; thus—

1st सुटल + तों = सुटलों I got loose.
2nd सुटल + तोस (or तास) = सुटलास Thougottest loose.
3rd सुटल + तो (or ता) = सुटला He got loose.

Note. ओ and आ are interchangeable in Maráṭhí, and indeed आ usually displaces ओ.

216. The past habitual forms are the oldest Maráṭhí tenses, and contain the greatest Sanskṛit element. The other Maráṭhí tenses could be easily traced to them.

The habitual tenses have two classes of forms, corresponding to the Sanskṛit Á'tmanepad and the Parasmaipad forms. The Maráṭhí verbs of the first conjugation take the Á'tmanepad terminations, and those of the second conjugation take the terminations of the Parasmaipad. Thus—

FIRST CONJUGATION.

1st Sing. ए S. = मि Prák. = एं M. (सुट + एं = सुटें).
2nd ,, से S. = से Prák. = एस or अस M. (सुट + एस = सुटेस).
3rd ,, ते S. = ए Prák. = ए M. (सुट + ए = सुटे).
1st Plu. महे S. = मु Prák. = ऊं M. (सुट + ऊं = सुटूं).
2nd ,, ध्वे S. = ह Prák. = आ M. (सुट + आ = सुटा).
3rd ,, अते S. = अति Prák. = अति or अत M. (सुट + अत = सुटत).

Note. ह and आ are interchangeable, just as the Visarga; ओ and आ are interchangeable.

Note. The Anusvára on तों (1st sing. present), and the स in तोस (2nd sing. present) are immediately derived from the habitual forms सुटें and सुटस.

SECOND CONJUGATION.

1st Sing. मि S. = मि Prák. = ईं (सोड + ईं = सोडीं).
2nd „ सि S. = सि Prák. = सि or ईस (सोडी + ईस = सोडीस).
3rd „ ति S. = ति Prák. = ई (सोड + इ = सोडी).
1st Plu. मः S. = मू Prák. = ऊं M. (साडे + ऊं = सोडूं).
2nd „ थ S. = ह Prák. = आ M. (सोड + आ = सोडा).
3rd „ अन्ति S. = अति Prák. = ईत M. (सोड + ईत = सोडीत).

217. The future Maráthí forms are identical with the past habitual forms, the slight difference between them being easily explained. Thus—

	1st Conj.		2nd Conj.	
	P. H.	F.	P. H.	F.
1st Sing.	ए	= एन ;	ईं	= ईन
2nd „	एस or अस	= सोल ;	ईस	= सोल
3rd „	ए	= एल ;	ई	= ईल.
1st Plu.	ऊं	= ऊं ;	ऊं	= ऊं
2nd „	आ	= आल ;	आ	= आल
3rd „	अत	= तोल ;	ईत	= तोल

Note. The reason why the habitual and the future forms are alike is this, that in Sanskrit the future personal endings are identical with the present, excepting the double letter ष्य which distinguishes the future.

Note. The ल in the Maráthí future forms is probably a modification of the Prákṛit द or दि substituted for the Sanskrit ति; and द and ल are interchangeable letters: thus, करिष्यति He will do (S.), करिस्सदि (Prák.), करोल (M.). The future ष्य or इस being dropt, दि or ति is left, and the vowel being dropt, द or त is left: this त or द is the Maráthí ल.

218. *The Conditional Mood.*

The inflections of the conditional are like those of the indicative present.

219. *The Subjunctive Mood.*

The subjunctive mood is formed by adding the suffix आवें to the verbal root. आवें is derived from the Sanskrit subjunctive इयं, which is modified in the dual to इव, and in the plural to इम. The Sanskrit य is, sometimes, changed in Prákrit to व, and आवें could therefore be easily identified with इवं; thus ज्ञानियं S. = जाणवं = Prák. जाणवें I may know. यं is changed to यां in some Sanskrit forms, which in Prákrit would be वां or आवां.

220. *The Imperative Mood.*

The imperative terminations are thus derived:—

Sing. 1st   आनि S. = मु Prák. = ऊं M.
 ,,   2nd   अ   S. = अ   ,,   = अ   ,,
 ,,   3rd   तु   S. = उ   ,,   = उ or ओ M. (सुट्+उ = सुटू.)
Plu. 1st   अम   S. = मो   ,,   = ऊं M. (सुट्+ऊं = सुटूं.)
 ,,   2nd   त   S. = ह   ,,   = आ M. (सुट्+आ = सुटा.)
 ,,   3rd   न्तु S. = अन्तु ,,   = ऊत or ओत M. (सुट्+ओत, सुटोत.)

Note. These Sanskrit terminations of the imperative mood pertain to the Parasmaipad, but they are related to Maráṭhí verbs of both the first and second conjugations.

221. *The Infinitive Mood.*

The infinitive termination ऊं is derived from the Sanskrit तुं, changed in Prákrit to दुं or उं;—मया गन्तुं शक्यते I can go, मी जाऊं शकतों; कृष्णं द्रष्टुं व्रजति He goes to see Krishṇa.

222. *The Participles.*

The present participles in त, तां, and तांना are all derived from the Sanskrit present participial bases, अंतृ and अंत्. In some forms the तृ is changed to न्; as अदन्.

The past participles in ला or लेला are derived from the past participle passive suffix त: or न: m., changed in Prákrit to दो. The dentals and ल are interchangeable; thus कृनः S. केलेला; कृना S. केलेलो; कृनें S. केलेलें done.

The future participle णार is the corruption of the Sanskrit future participial suffix मानः or भानः ; as बुध्यमानः = जाणणार knower, मोक्ष-मानः = सोडणारा looser.

223. *The Gerund.*

The gerundial termination णें is the modification of the Sanskrit अन and the Prákrit णं; श्रु S. to hear = श्रवणं = सणं Prák. = ऐकणें; सोवनं (S.), सोवणा Prak., सिवणें to sew.

APPENDIX.

NOTE I.

The grammatical forms which occur in old Maráthí poetry, sometimes, differ from those given in this work, and a few of the principal of them are here subjoined :—

DECLENSION OF THE NOUNS.

ईश्वर God.

१	ईश्वर	५	ईश्वरापासुनि-पासुनियां
२	ईश्वरा-प्रत		ईश्वराहुनि-हुनियां
३	ईश्वरें, ईश्वरेशीं		ईश्वरापासाव
४	{ ईश्वरा { ईश्वरालागीं-लागुनि	६	ईश्वराचा, as -चेनि as -चिया
		७	ईश्वरीं.

OBLIQUE CASE OF ADJECTIVES.

चांगल्याचिया -चियें -चेनी.

PRONOUNS.

In Prákṛit हे, ते, जे are used for ही, ती, जी, and जया and तया for ह्या and त्या.

मातें is the 2nd case of मी, and तूतें of तूं.

VERBS.

The following form serves for the present and past, and, sometimes, for the future indicative :—

Intransitive Verb उठणें To rise.   Transitive Verb करणें To do.

	Singular.	Plural.	Singular.	Plural.
1.	मी उठें	आम्हीं उठूं	मीं करीं	आम्हीं करूं
2.	तूं उठस	तुम्हीं उठा	तूं करीस	तुम्हीं करा
3.	तो, ती, तें उठे	ते, त्या, तीं उठती.	तो, ती, तें करी.	ते, त्या, तीं करितो.

Imperative Mood.

तूं उठ   तूं करि

Pluperfect Participle.

उठोनि उठुनि.   करोनि करुनि.

The following tenses, with जे inserted after the root, are used both actively and passively, but properly in the latter mode; thus मो मारिजे तों I am struck.

	Singular. m. f. n.	Plural.
Present Kartari Prayoga.	मो करिजे तों-ने-तों ने करिजेतोस-तीस-तेंस तो, तो, तें, करिजेतों- ती-ने	आम्हो करिजेतों तुम्हीं करिजेता ते, स्या, तीं करिजेतान

	Singular.	Plural.	
Present Bhávi Prayoga.	म्या त्वा त्यानें, तिनें	आम्हीं तुम्हीं त्यानीं	करिजेतें
Past Karmani Prayoga and Bhávi Prayoga.	म्या त्वा त्यानें, तिनें	आम्हीं तुम्हीं त्यानीं	करिजेला -ली-लें-ले-ल्या-लीं
Future Bhávi Prayoga.	म्या त्वा त्यानें तिनें	आम्हीं तुम्हीं त्यानीं	करिजेल
Imperative.	त्वा करिजे	तुम्हीं करिजे	
Past Participle.	करिजेला-ली-लें		

(*Stevenson's Grammar.*)

NOTE II.

PARSING.

ते गरीब आहेत. (They are poor.)

ते   is a pers. pronoun of the 3rd pers., the plu. number, the mas. gender, and in the nom. case to "आहेत."

गरीब   is an adj. of quality, qualifying ते.

आहेन is a subs. verb, ind. mood, pres. tense, and the 3rd pers. sing. mas., agreeing with its nominative तें. It is of the subjective construction, because it agrees with the subject in gender and number.

रामानें तुमची कुचेष्टा केली असावी.

रामानें is a proper noun of the 1st declension, of the 3rd. pers., the sing. number, the mas. gender, and in the instrumental case of agency, nominative to केली असावी.

तुमची is a personal pronoun, of the 2nd pers., the plu. number, and the genitive case, governed by the feminine noun कुचेष्टा.

कुचेष्टा is a common noun of the 3rd declension, of the 3rd pers., the sing. number, fem. gend., and in the accusative case governed by केली असावी.

केली असावी is an irreg. trans. verb, subjunctive mood, past tense (dubitative), the 3rd pers. sing. fem., and has for its nominative रामानें. It is in the objective construction, since it agrees with its object कुचेष्टा.

मला बोलावयास कोणीं शिकविलें.

मला is a pers. pronoun * * * and is in the dative case, expressing the direct object.

बोलायास is the dative supine.

कोणीं is an interrogative pronoun in the instrumental case of agency, being nominative to शिकविलें.

शिकविलें is a reg. causal verb, indic. mood, past tense, the 3rd pers. sing. neut., and has for its nominative कोणीं. It is in the neuter construction. Repeat the rule.

BOMBAY: PRINTED AT THE EDUCATION SOCIETY'S PRESS, BYCULLA.

www.ingramcontent.com/pod-product-compliance
Lightning Source LLC
Chambersburg PA
CBHW030350170426
43202CB00010B/1328